STUCK IN THE DOOR

A memoir from 34 years in and out of 12 step fellowships

MARILYN COOPER

"Someone has to be strong;
it might as well be YOU"

The Author;

I am not a therapist, counsellor or health professional. My story describes my own personal experiences in AA and a treatment centre. All names, places and events have been altered to maintain anonymity and safety of all concerned. Self-awareness has been the key to my own "revival"; I sincerely hope that you may find yours.

Marliyn Cooper

Contents

Preface..

Introduction..

- Chapter 1   Critical Mass
- Chapter 2   Drip, drip, drip
- Chapter 3   The 13th Step
- Chapter 4   In treatment
- Chapter 5   You have a disease
- Chapter 6   The AA way of life
- Chapter 7   Keep coming back/relapse
- Chapter 8   The AA Couple
- Chapter 9   Promises, promises
- Chapter 10   Recovered
- Chapter 11   Unlearning
- Chapter 12   Trauma
- Chapter 13   Awareness

Preface

"You can do what you will; I will exist regardless, but remember; there will never be another quite like me when I have gone"

Firstly, don't be cruel to yourself for falling for the brainwashing. If you came, as I did, from an emotionally stunted family, then you weren't in a great position to see the manipulation and dogma coming at you. Particularly as you were extremely vulnerable. Suggestibility is the signature wound of the vulnerable.

AA trades fully and wholeheartedly on that premise, and this book on my own personal experiences and "time" in AA and other 12 step fellowship programmes is part of a growing global avalanche of stories from a huge variety of people; young, old, rich, poor, addicted/not addicted who want to get their voices heard.

It is a long overdue response to the decades of media/celebrity friendly propaganda that has washed over the world since "The Big Book" of AA came into being in 1930's depression era America. Those of us who have "lived the programme" are flying out of the closet faster than a camisole in a 1970's Janet Reger knicker sale. And that really dates me as a 64-year-old woman from the UK, working class with upwardly mobile desires in underwear.

I was 30 years old when I got involved in AA, treatment, and "the programme". I got sober on my own and stayed that way for 6 months before I met someone who went to meetings and suggested I go and "listen". I had lived in London for 5 years in the late 70's and 80's and my drinking had really taken off, helped by my job in Public Relations as a company journalist, a profession well-known and ribbed for its propensity to keep the alcohol industry in bonuses.

I had moved back to Bristol and my life was falling off the edges of any reality I had managed to adhere to, and I had what some "old-timers" called "a eureka moment". They called it God; I call it inner awakening. I am not religious, I have explored many religions and practices and I believe the closest I feel to any practice is mysticism. Each to her own. AA is, first and foremost, a religious organisation, despite its continual vehement protestations.

 Many people are questioning everything at this point in history, particularly in the light of the Covid pandemic, which continues as I write. During the Zoom Meeting era of AA, literally thousands of members began to challenge this "programme" that they had followed, quite slavishly in many instances, and were not happy with what now seemed hollow and dogmatic. I was one of them.

I left in Summer 2021 after 34 years in and out of the programme. I don't credit AA with my sobriety anymore; in fact, for 13 years in the middle of that 34 year period I went to no meetings at all and lived very well with regular psychotherapy sessions whilst bringing up my daughter.

To some reading this, that may sound ungrateful and egotistical (yes, if you have been in the programme, you will know exactly what guilt buttons are being pressed). If you have no experience of fellowship programmes then I ask you to keep an open mind and plough ahead with this book; you may recognise yourself a little and come to the realization that it isn't idiots who get brainwashed; it is ordinary everyday people, just like me, just like you.

I believe self-awareness, continued good counselling/ trauma therapy, trusted friends and self-education and creative outlets are paramount in changing your life for the better if you have abused alcohol or any other substances/activities in order to dull the pain of your own personal hell. This can begin at any time and it is never too late.

There are numerous other ways to "stay clean/abstinent" or to moderate alcohol use (I believe you should be able to call it what you will, and also refuse to be "labelled" by professionals/groups if you feel it is detrimental to your own definition of self) and there is much credible evidence supporting scientific approaches to alcohol/drug misuse now available. You do not need a god, a religion or a sponsor to find good health. Working at life, for me, is a natural process, involving mistakes, successes, pitfalls, outside help and inner reflection, and ultimately following my intuition.

This story is my own, based on real experiences. Names and places have been changed to respect confidentiality, my own included. However, I portray AA as I see it, and I am certain this will upset rigid "12 steppers" everywhere.

 It's about time. This book is aimed at anyone with a doubt, or many doubts who is still in the programme; it is aimed at health professionals, media workers, therapists, in fact anyone who really needs to know that AA is not the benign, benevolent structure that is so often depicted in TV shows and in the news.

More and more Hollywood celebrities are presenting as "recovering alcoholics/addicts" – and you can guess how that network operates when the top jobs are going! AA is a school tie network, just like any other and its power is wide and far reaching. It is deserving of close examination and scrutiny, as all registered charities should be.

If you have recently left AA after a long, or even a short sojourn in "the rooms", I've got a suggestion for you before you start reading Chapter 1. Write down a list of all the good things you have done for yourself without AA. You'll find it's a refreshingly full list; your own experiences and intuition are your best friends; not a group of people who collectively insist that you reiterate your powerlessness at every meeting.

I write with love and regard for everything you have experienced and all the growth to come.

Marilyn Cooper, 2022

Nb. In this work I will use AA terminology for the purposes of explanation (many people do not know the extensive "coded" language of AA, though more phrases and slogans are slipping into common usage.) I will use quotation marks to denote the AA references in the body of the text.

Introduction

"Nowhere in the dozens of books and pamphlets published by AA will you find even a hint that there is any cause of alcoholism (or even contributory factors), other than the alcoholic him/herself"

(Charles Bufe, "Cult or Cure?" See Sharp Press 1998).

Wellness is my aim. I don't have a system; I certainly don't have a "programme" anymore. I am open minded to all experience, and I have learned to turn off my "always open" neon sign. I am abstinent from alcohol; however, if people can drink alcohol and live a decent, kind, responsible life then I have no problem with that.

My friends and supportive others are from many walks of life, are differing ages, have a variety of skills and interests; some drink, some don't.

I'm approaching my story at a recent point and will ping-pong on the timeline of my life, basically because it's how my brain works best. Luckily, I was able to retain my critical faculties to a great extent whilst in AA. I believe this explains why I

had a problem fully accepting the programme from day one – 34 plus years ago.

I am and always will be a free-thinker. It has helped me to survive and stay sane in what was and is a very toxic organisation.

Re-read the Charles Bufe quote at the start of this introduction, taken from his excellent, well-researched book.

In essence AA is a blame game. YOU did this to yourself, with no contributory factors! This simplistic approach has definitely caused more despair, depression and "relapse" than any other single piece of AA propaganda.

It is designed to promote helplessness, fear and a victim mentality. It negates all trauma-based experience and family/societal pressures that have harmed the individual. It is not helpful, particularly in early "recovery" or drink/harm reduction.

A rounded, considered picture of a person's life is the foundation of all good therapeutic work – not taking one strand in isolation and focusing entirely on that strand. To encourage healthy development and healing of a fractured personality/lifestyle, ALL experiences and behaviours need to be encompassed in the process. This includes help from trained professionals.

What results from one-stranded thinking? One-stranded "recovery"- hence the ongoing deep depressions, self-hatred, sense of failure and unlived lives prevalent amongst many AA members.

Yet the insistence of the AA message "the only way to stay sober is to keep coming back" is continually affirmed, at every meeting, by members old and new. There is no real evidence for that claim. What exists is a euphoric, magical thinking carpet of repetition, dogma and religion (masked as spirituality).

I have heard AA members (countless times) proudly say such things as "I stopped therapy, I gave up all my old friends, my old playgrounds (some of them useful!), my meds (without advice or help from a doctor) and put all my faith and trust in the programme and I haven't looked back!"

Reflection, other than confessional re-runs of "bad behaviour" is not considered useful in AA Land. It's better to believe in the little green wizard behind the curtain who has no idea what he is doing…..

At the start of my de-programming, (i.e., making concerted continual efforts to let go of cult-thinking, language and lifestyles) I was still attending AA meetings via Zoom. My "fireside group" in CODA (a format popular in rural areas where members live far apart), had disbanded after mutual agreement. We had been a small group of 4 regulars.

That group experience was far kinder than any AA one I'd had and I remain in close contact with 2 members. The four of us had questioned and discussed relationship issues way beyond the scope of a traditional CODA meeting; I'm pretty certain any service representative of the CODA fellowship would have been horrified at our interpretation of their programme!

I had also been shielding due to Stage 4 cancer/stem cell transplant all of 2019/20 which was a major "trigger" event that led me to reassess my life and my connections with AA and fellowship programmes. Then Covid hit the world and AA meetings went to Zoom. This meant a new way of being in a meeting (I hadn't been to a physical meeting for a very long time due to my clinical vulnerability status in cancer recovery (- note that I do not put recovery in quotes in this instance; cancer is a real illness; alcoholism is not.)

I didn't go to Zoom meetings for at least 6 months at the start of Covid, then one day I thought I'd give it a try. This stepping back from AA had given me time to be my self without the intervention of a programme. I felt fine, but the many years of brainwashing kicked in and I found an ID and password for my local home group and plunged back in.

It was then that I started to see things, to hear things; to listen to my inner voice in a new way. I was trained as a journalist and so I began surreptitiously taking notes in the meetings. I felt one step removed. People were talking, heads were nodding, but it felt like a horrible dream, a completely inauthentic experience. A lot of it was shocking, but I realised that I heard it all before, over the years, at thousands of AA meetings.

I was waking up from the fog. When you are physically present in a meeting and participating in the jargon and the group-think, it is hard to understand what is actually going on. My new "sitting back" stance gave me pause to reflect on what was being said and I would later read back my notes in astonishment.

It gave me the opportunity to read the sub-text (something I had been taught to do in Drama of Theatre at college and which now became extremely useful). The shaming language, the shut-down techniques of "old-timers" (long-standing AA members) when someone went "off-programme", the self-flagellating approach to "recovery", the dismissal of real, lived experience of painful traumatic events (sometimes in a trite sentence or sometimes by ignoring the speaker, or rapidly changing the subject).

It felt liberating not to be in a real room with these people anymore; the virtual reality of it gave me mental freedom. It was also horrifying as my awareness grew.

A real eye-opener, to use a cliché, but AA has plenty of those too! I am so glad I began my exit from AA at that time (Summer 2021) and began to unravel the gordian knot that AA had become for me.

I reiterate that this is my story, my experience and I am writing it partly to exorcise the whole damned programme mentality from my world, but also to give perspective and help to counter the media love affair that US/UK society has with AA and other 12 step fellowship programmes.

 I mis-typed that as fellowshop to begin with – maybe that is a more accurate term for them when you understand that addiction is a multi-million-pound medical model that brings huge financial rewards for its shareholders, through treatment centres worldwide.

Also, I want my daughter and step-son and all younger people to really take a long look at these programmes and get all the information they can on them and not get hoodwinked by pseudo-religious slogans instead of the real professional help they may need.

AA is a cult. It is a self-perpetuating hydra that has held many in thrall for decades. There are alternatives; there is a shed load of scientific evidence and research now, easily available via the internet that gives hope and offers different methods of dealing with alcohol/drug misuse.

There is also the fact (one you will never hear in an AA meeting) that many people reach a natural "dead-end" with their drinking/using and get sober/clean with the help of friends, therapy, lifestyle changes, a new relationship or career switch, with no hint of any programme.

Worryingly, many young people (they seem to get younger) are being labelled as alcoholics/addicts in their teens; the natural stage of experimentation amongst human beings the world over since time began. If someone becomes an "alcoholic" at, for example, 19 years of age and is indoctrinated into the programme of AA, how easy it will then be for ANY authoritarian structure to control that compliant person? If they have serious trauma-based issues underlying their drinking/drugging, they will not get that help in the cult of AA. They will be taught to follow 12 religious steps and to pray to a Higher Power to save them.

"Suspend your critical thinking" is one slogan you will not see pinned up in an AA meeting room.

I do not identify as an alcoholic anymore. I had a drinking problem. It's over, cured by self-help, help from others and time. Labels are not useful when you are able to work things out for yourself, when you come to terms with what makes you tick and your inner potential. Many people, doubtless will disagree with that statement. I don't mean the idiocy of not identifying such conditions as diabetes, epilepsy or autism. I am talking about the commonality of reclaiming one's self and identity from a dogmatic structure that has a vested interest in keeping you sick and hidden from yourself.

I've turned off the programme. Normal service is resuming.

Marilyn Cooper, Spring 2022.

Chapter 1
Critical Mass

I think that a web of interconnecting traumatic events (many dating from childhood) form the crucial build-up that leads to critical mass – when something's got to give.

My significant moment came when I was 30. I had returned to Bristol from London after a fun and fairly lucrative time as a company journalist for two major corporations in the late 70's/early 80's and, at age 25 was feeling pretty rudderless in Thatcher's Britain.

 The early death of my boss in London, who had mentored me and was instrumental in getting me involved in politics and a social conscience had been devastating. A lovely man, taken far too early at age 51, this was an event that shook me.

Back in Bristol, I lived with my boyfriend and I got involved in music, bands, heavier drinking (I was well-practiced as a writer in London), drugs, politics, poetry; not quite sure what I wanted or where I was going. I wanted to let my hair down, especially after all the stress of London and the sadness I left behind.

At age 28 I had a miscarriage; my partner was a musician with equally heavy drinking habits and the loss of our child brought the rocky relationship to an end. We had propped each other up in our drinking and drifting lifestyles and though there was a lot of love between us, there was very little maturity.

Depression and loneliness followed, accompanied by heavier drinking as I tried to get some solid anchors in my life. But I couldn't. Looking back, I can see how very vulnerable I was; overwhelmed with sadness, loss, despair and uncertainty.

 My family were of little help; they had been young parents themselves and now they were both middle aged they wanted to enjoy the fun life they hadn't had whilst they had been bringing up children and working hard. I was close to my father, but not to my mother, and my sister had always hated me.

 Our family had been fairly insular when I was growing up; we had no real connections with an extended family and I always felt we were apart from our relatives. I have done a great amount of therapy around my family of origin, and I will refer to relevant parts of that when necessary. Suffice to say I was pretty fucked up and I didn't have a very solid template for living.

I began going to free singing groups, new-age workshops, spiritualist meetings – I was seeking and searching, on a budget. My lucrative earning period had come to an abrupt halt when I returned to Bristol and I was surviving on the dole and bar jobs, all the time getting involved with bands and musicians, because I realised, I wanted to perform my songs and try and make a living from it.

I was hoping to find a structure that would help me re-build my life. I stopped drinking when the drunken boyfriend I was with tried to strangle me. I haven't had a drink since that day over 34 years ago.

So, I was looking for new friends, new connections both musical and workwise; I had plenty of fire in me, but it was severely dampened by the undealt with grief and trauma issues from my past.

I met Derek at a free singing workshop (paid for by the Job Centre – yes, really! This was the 80's, there were free workshops and training for the unemployed!). There was a host of good stuff on offer for free in those days and I took advantage of whatever I thought would help.

Many attending came from the ranks of the damaged; drinkers, drug takers, long term unemployed people, the outsiders, the "tatterdemalion beggars" of society, of which I proudly counted myself one. I'd had more than enough of corporate life. I felt at home there.

Derek played percussion and I took an instant, powerful liking to him – it was an addictive compulsive attraction in every way. I felt lonely, I wanted something new, I was scared to be alone, the reasons are legion, and many who have given up drinking will understand the chasm left when the booze is gone. And he was sober (a new term to me), and he was in AA and NA. I didn't even know what that meant at the time. He seemed full of fun and lightness and the word was that he had "beaten addiction" and had 3 years sobriety. He was held in high esteem by the group, quite a few of whom were in "recovery". I'd been sober, under my own steam, for 4 months. His 3 years seemed like a monumental achievement and I too looked up to him.

He was also extremely damaged, but because of my own messed up head, I couldn't see that; I didn't *want* to see that!

We started a sexual relationship almost immediately and from the very start I wanted to dive into this new world of AA, meetings and community. Different people, places and things were on offer, I saw it as an opportunity to change my life for the better and begin again, without the drinking that had brought me so low. At no point at this stage was I calling myself an alcoholic.

I went to London with him for a weekend; it was where he had been brought up (he was of American/Balkan origin and his mother still lived there; she too was in recovery and it was only later that I discovered that Derek had gone to Al-a-teen as young man to help him come to terms with his mother's alcoholism. So, he was a "programme kid" from the get go).

We went to several AA meetings; one very big one somewhere near the Kings Road sticks in my memory. It was weird. I felt overwhelmed by so many people; loud, laughing, smoking constantly (AA/NA was still tobacco central; I hated it, having been a non-smoker all my life). I went into a "freeze" mode, something which I always reverted to when I felt extremely anxious – part of my childhood trauma.

Luckily, I was only expected to "sit and listen to the similarities, not the differences. Close your mouth and open your ears". What an odd thing to say! I thought to myself. It was like nothing I had ever heard before; men and women of all ages were disclosing private, sometimes intimate information about their lives, and I didn't feel at all comfortable. That was my inner intuition giving me a very big nudge, but at the time, I wasn't really listening.

After the meeting (which ended with a short prayer which took me by total surprise) Derek chatted to numerous people whom he seemed to know really well, hugging everyone as if they were long-lost friends re-encountered after an extended sea-voyage. I felt bewildered and tried to stay "small". One of his friends, a guy in his twenties asked me what I had thought of the meeting.

I thought he wanted my true response, so I said I thought it was OK, but I didn't like the religion and I thought people really needed to have practical help to get well and learn to rely on themselves rather than a "programme". I opined that AA could "easily become a crutch rather than a support if you went for too long".

His jaw dropped and his eyes glazed over, and I could sense an anger building in his body as his face flushed red. "NO, that's not it at all! Hey, you're new, Derek will soon get you on the programme; ask him about it. Nice to meet you!" he said and quickly left my side. I felt as if I had done something terrible, said something that had caused incredible offence. I wanted Derek's' new friends to like me, and here I was, blundering through my first meeting causing chaos.

I sat and waited till Derek had said hello to everyone (and I mean everyone) and I looked forward to getting him to myself so we could enjoy our Saturday afternoon visiting old London haunts we were both familiar with, hanging out in book shops, record stores, maybe go to a movie……but no…. seven of the AA group were going for coffee, and we were invited to join them.

I really didn't want to go, but I felt vulnerable and unable to ask for what I wanted. Also, my confidence around Derek was low and I didn't want to upset him (red flag, but in those days, I had no idea)

What followed was a tedious 3-hour continuation of the AA meeting; the coffee and cake was good, I remember that! The conversation went from programme issues to people who had "relapsed" (I didn't know what that meant), the merits of different treatment centres – one of the group had been in treatment in America and received shiny eyed stares.

Then there was excited mention of an "annual convention" that was being held soon in London, and Derek immediately piped up to say he was going. A young woman, Ann, asked me if I was going too. I quickly said I didn't think so. Mostly, I was ignored, I'm shy by nature, particularly with groups of people I don't know well. I was left to my thoughts which were intense and convoluted as I struggled to understand what was being said and what these people were about.

Were they religious? There were prayers and many mentions of God at the meeting…. What the fuck are they talking about? What else do they do in their lives? No one has mentioned a job or musical interests or books they are reading…. They were all well-heeled – I learned fairly quickly that AA/12 step groups are a class based societal structure.

I'm working-class, but I've mixed in all social/economic groups due to working firstly as a corporate journalist and secondly as a singer performer. I don't get phased by people who think they are above me. I just try to get on with the person in front of me; something my Dad was great at and I learned, in part from him.

What was this "coded language" they were all speaking? What was a Step 4 and what constituted character defects? Had they all been to prison? Were they all part of some sort of government funded social experiment that I didn't know about?

It felt like I had walked into a secret society that viewed itself as different from the normal lifestyles I was used to. No one seemed "real" to me. From that day to this, I have felt the same. Of course, I have asked myself why I stayed so long. I've let myself off the hook on that score. I needed to find out what made me tick, and this new group seemed a way of taking a different path in life.

I've always been open, a seeker, looking for meaning – plus I had no job, no drinking buddies anymore and nothing else to do! (Or so I thought at the time) I wanted a sense of community, some new people around me and of course I craved acceptance and love – that is the bait that keeps you coming back as with any cult structure.

This is very important to my story. I was a vulnerable person with psychological/alcohol misuse issues; when I found myself with no purpose, no aim, I tended to fill the gaps with whatever was available to distract me from the emptiness and pain of my existence; it is a commonality amongst trauma survivors.

I no longer feel a need to do this, I haven't felt like that for many years. This has taken a great deal of reflection, therapy, personal growth and simply…. time. That's not to say I couldn't have done with some alternative help to AA sooner!

AA seemed like a new start to me; a new set of friends who were all working on themselves (on reflection, I see they were STUCK) and who wanted to help others "achieve sobriety". I love language, I'm a writer after all, and I quickly latched on to the slogans, the platitudes, the homilies; this was part of the code and I was willing to learn!

I could never stomach "The Big Book" (I've never owned a copy) – it seemed badly written, misogynistic, quaint and outdated. Plain ridiculous in places! I wondered what the fuss was about regarding the "book". Surely there were better books on addiction and the psychology of misuse? I've been an avid reader my entire life and at that time was reading Jung, Freud, Adler, Alice Miller amongst other works. This "Big Book" was embarrassing in its simplicity!

I was quickly told that was my ego talking, my intellectual side that couldn't grasp the purity of the "message" I tried to understand that, but secretly I thought "why is AA stuck with the Big Book as a frame of reference when the issues people face are so tough and need practical answers?"

I began a double-life. I wanted to fit in. I wanted the relationship with Derek. I wanted a measure of mental security that I thought was on offer in AA. Over the first 3 years, I became good "newcomer" material for the fellowship. I did shares, I took posts (tea making, literature secretary, meeting chair) and I went to a 12-step treatment centre (after 6 months sobriety and on the express instruction of Derek who said I needed it. Primarily, I went to please him)

Interestingly, the main thing that I got from treatment was that it got me away from Derek's influence for 11 weeks and I was able to start looking at myself as an individual apart from him. There were many downsides too, which I will explore in a later chapter. In fact, treatment was the beginning of the end of my relationship with Derek.

How this came about provides a good illustration of the sickness of much AA interaction. At the meetings in Bristol, I had struck up a friendship with a woman, Jane, who was slightly longer in sobriety than me. She was also a good friend of Derek's.

Whilst in treatment, I constantly questioned why I was even there (I still do). I'd been sober for 6 months before going in and I had felt my life was getting better. Such is the nature of compliance and suggestibility in a vulnerable individual.

Whilst I was in "primary care" (8 weeks at that time), Jane rang me and wrote to me, she even visited me one Sunday (visiting day) telling me how "courageous" I was.

Meanwhile "on the outside" she had developed a close bond with Derek, meeting him for coffee, providing a shoulder to cry on whilst his girlfriend was in treatment. Poor Derek! I had no idea this was happening until someone "leaked" it to me. I felt utterly betrayed and humiliated. Jane had been my ally, a rock of fellowship stability, someone who said they had my back and who I could trust when I "got out".

Derek said nothing in his defence; he could see no problems with his behaviour (he never could; one of the reasons why we split up of course).

My betrayal felt complete when I eventually arranged to meet Jane after leaving treatment. She would only consent to seeing me with her sponsor present and she sat in stony silence while I spilled out my pain, hurt and sadness (as I had been so recently trained to do in treatment). It was one of the most degrading experiences in early recovery, the first of many as I progressed in AA. Thankfully, I did not drink. I was determined not to.

After Derek and I broke up, I really felt I was on my own again. I adhered to AA more fully, chairing meetings and sharing regularly. I did a meeting, sometimes 2 every day, walking miles around Bristol to attend a variety of meetings. I had no car but I had tons of angry energy to fuel my journeys.

I tried to get a sponsor. In fact, I had two attempts with sponsors before I realised, I just wouldn't be able to be told what to do by these women who had no idea who I really was, showed no inclination to get to know me on any other level than an "alcoholic" one, and who had no qualifications other than they drank too much, just like I had.

Here is my first experience of sponsorship. She was a middle-aged single woman with 25 years sober time. After a big Saturday night meeting, we went for coffee. (It had been a "microphone meeting", very well attended. I shared there several times in early recovery and I cringe when I think of the inappropriate self-disclosure I displayed; sometimes to applause!). Incidentally, this meeting was a playground for predators of all persuasions.

She listened to my innocent ramblings about feeling glad to have stopped drinking, and I mistook her silent, brooding presence for approval as I became excited about my new musical/poetry project that was in the offing, and enthused about the renewed hopes and dreams I had for the future (I was 30 at this time).

When I stopped talking, she suddenly looked very piteously at me (this is a very particular AA look that I have witnessed on many occasions) and said "Marilyn, those hopes and dreams are what keep you sick. They are not grounded in reality – it is your disease talking. You need to focus on working the steps now and let go of all that other life. I once felt like you, but it's not real!" I felt utterly deflated and ashamed.

When I look back, I remember thinking; "she's a middle-aged miserable woman who is scared and jealous of my enthusiasm because it reminds her of her lost dreams". I haven't changed that view in 34 years. I never went for coffee with her again and sacked her, by phone, the next day. I had good intuition and a sense of self-preservation even in my lowest moments at that time. Such heartless comments and unkind, critical behaviour are very commonplace amongst "sponsors". I saw more of it as I became part of the AA community. I tried "co-sponsoring" later on in AA, but that was not successful either. It became a chore to ring this woman up every time I had a decision to make or a problem to solve; or to "share feelings". Also, I had chosen a woman who strongly resembled my mother in character and temper. This was never going to work; I was choosing from a place of unawareness, which would change as I worked with trauma issues with my therapist. Sponsor number 2 was let go of, rather quickly.

Chapter 2
Drip, drip, drip....

In AA there are many platitudes, slogans and phrases that are endlessly repeated. Thankfully, zoom meetings during the Covid pandemic meant that these slogans, that normally adorn the walls of meeting rooms, were no longer in evidence.

After over 30 years in "the rooms" it is still taking me time to eliminate them from my consciousness. The simplistic nature of slogans can be very powerful, I can compare it to the "hook" in a song, the words you remember, the emotional "grab" that gets you every time.

When I gave up drinking, my clarity of thought came back very quickly. The neuroplasticity of the brain (at any age) is astonishing – we are retraining ourselves constantly. If we wish, we can focus on healthy change and individuation (the aim of the mature human being). Worthwhile input is essential in early "recovery" from drinking/addiction issues.

For example, I accessed one-to-one counselling, I used AA (the fellowship meetings, at first, fell into the category of "support group" for me). AA, on the surface, offers identification, peer support, a safe haven. As I continued with fellowship meetings, these "promises" turned out to be hollow and also harmful to my progress.

In this chapter, I give my own interpretation on some of these slogans, looking at the sub-text, the underlying message that is designed to keep you hooked into "the programme" way of thinking. AA is a schoolroom for addicts; by turns authoritarian, paternalistic and misogynistic. It has a seductive, anarchic attraction ("our leaders are but trusted servants, they do not govern"). At the time, I thought it was revolutionary!

No leaders.... (Though Bill W. and Dr. Bob, the founders of AA are revered as heroes). "Our only requirement is to stop drinking. We have no dues or fees. We are not allied with any sect, denomination or creed" .... blah, blah, blah, naturally I can recite these lines without even thinking about them. That's an important fact. Much as I learn song or stage lines, I can use that part of my brain to recall the AA litany, which can also be tiresome.

The manifesto chimed well with me at the start. As with all organisations, the day to day lived reality is somewhat different. Discernment, the keystone of critical thinking, is missing from the Pollyanna platitudes of 12 step programmes.

In most cases, people join AA in very damaged, vulnerable conditions. We are looking for answers to our many questions about our difficult, fragmented lives and alcohol/drug misuse. Many of us were estranged from friends and family and had nowhere else to turn. When I joined AA in the late 80's, I had no idea there were any other forms of "recovery" for people with drink problems. AA was presented to me by the Alcohol Advisory Service as "the place to go".

From the first meeting, I did not find the slogans or the repetition particularly comforting, but I was willing to give AA a try as there was nothing else offered (though fortunately I got excellent long-term therapy from my local mental health team, something that is now extremely difficult to access for free).

Here, I offer a selection of AA phrases/slogans that have either been used in meetings or that I have heard spoken to other group members. I put my hand up to repeating many of these platitudes myself after years of brainwashing; for that, in reality, is what it is.

1."Look for the similarities, not the differences".

It is natural in a time of uncertainty and change to question new things and have critical thought processes. This platitude, used essentially on "newcomers" to AA encourages conformity/compliance as opposed to individuality.

2. *"We can do what I can't"*

The onus is on the group being able to solve your problems, irrespective of what they are. Practical steps taken by individuals to resolve chaotic life issues are often dismissed as "egotistical".

Yet each person has to leave the meeting at some point and live their life outside! I realise now how courageously and single mindedly many people I knew were dealing with very harsh life problems, yet in "the rooms" these efforts were dismissed or at best politely acknowledged. "Newcomers" are encouraged to believe that they cannot "do it alone". Dependency on AA is actively and relentlessly recommended from the outset.

3. *"There, for the Grace of God, go I"*

I find this phrase conjures up the German word "schadenfreude" for me; "look at that poor sod, I'm glad it's not me" It is also, obviously, a religious phrase. AA continually represents itself as a spiritual, not a religious programme. This is nonsense; AA is to all intents and purposes a religious programme.

4. "Hurt people hurt people"

Excuse your abusers; look for "your part" in it, accept all the damage as a learning curve and always forgive. No reflection, no in-depth discussion; a silly phrase to avoid real confrontation of painful events.

5. "One drink is too many and a thousand is never enough"

Evidence? There is none. Drunkalogues in AA meetings are always overblown. Some members describe Thor-like drinking from the legendary Horn of Plenty as regular occurrences. This "war-story" mentality is not only useless but incredibly destructive. It perpetuates the "powerless over alcohol" myth that upholds the AA structure.

Many heavy drinkers stop drinking alone, after weaning themselves off alcohol and have a spontaneous "remission" – and never go back, possibly due to life changes, therapy, a strong desire to improve ones' life because of the birth of a child or a marriage or a new career, or any number of reasons.

It happens to millions every day; personally achieved sobriety or abstinence/moderated drinking. Without AA. The constant threat of "jails, institutions and death" if you leave AA is a gothic monstrosity of a phrase. An anachronistic finger pointing permanently at the frightened "newcomers". Each person has different "recovery" needs; the one-size-fits-all model of AA is not working; in fact, it has never worked, and it is dangerous for many people.

6. *"Stinking thinking; (leads to drinking)"*

When I stopped drinking and began thinking clearly again, my mind was flooded with questions, deliberations, memories, anxieties, my head was in overdrive. I felt like a cup alternately filling and emptying.

AA seeks to stem this rediscovered awareness by labelling it with the pejorative tagline; "stinking thinking". Crass and unhelpful at best, dismissive of a persons' inner process at worst. I had in-depth therapy sessions with my local mental health team, over a period of 6 years during which I worked on core trauma issues.

Many AA members questioned me in a very invasive manner about this. "Why do you need that? AA has all you need; don't get lost in the psychobabble – they don't understand!" was the general gist of the attack. Yet, it was at this juncture, with intensive therapy, that I felt my "real recovery" began to emerge.

I still went regularly to AA and Coda (codependents anonymous, a 12-step fellowship based on the same principles as AA and dealing specifically with "unhealthy" dependency issues). I felt like I was living parallel lives. One foot in AA and one foot in my new reality without drink.

7. *"Recovery is 1% me and 99% everyone else"*

All your efforts, your lived experience, your struggles for growth and change and your achievements are all down to – everyone else! But mainly to God, your higher power.

I did not believe in God and was never comfortable with the "handing over" business as it meant absolutely nothing to me.

I saw good people in "the rooms" as well as bad; I saw everyone desperately trying to "make it" via a set of outdated religious pointers with varying success. Take the sting out of this simplistic slogan for good. Your power is within.

This slogan is often used by the "old-timers", yet they are the very people who find it very difficult to actually listen to anyone's real experience!

8. "The Newcomer is the most important person in the room"

A clever phrase that "lovebombs" the vulnerable newcomers and "right sizes" old-timers, whose job it is to package the programme as the panacea to all the problems that come with sobriety.

Some truth and caring does leak through from the group, particularly when you are a "newbie", fresh to the fellowship programme. But it doesn't last. Overwhelming feelings, broken friendships/relationships, home life changes, illness, bankruptcy and financial troubles, poor mental health – all these and many more conditions cannot be addressed by a fellowship that suggests prayer as an infallible solution to your practical problems.

Yet the group insists that this is true, and when people fail (which they regularly do) it is deemed to be their fault as they "didn't get the programme". Victim blaming 100%.

9. Righteous anger is a luxury the alcoholic cannot afford"

If you have been in the fellowship and are reading this, I can almost hear you all seething and hissing at this one! Access to my anger has, literally, kept me alive, no question about that. Firstly, it is a normal human response to ill-treatment or a dangerous situation, and secondly it has usually been inordinately suppressed in people who misuse alcohol and drugs. It has to come out, regularly and authentically and not be rejected. It's a hugely important part of the tool-kit we need, particularly women putting their lives back together after abuse, dysfunction and years of low self-esteem in damaging situations.

We need our anger to fight for our rights, speak out against injustice, racism, cruelty, inequality. Integrated as part of our whole being, anger is a life-saver, not something to be ignored or repressed because it makes people uncomfortable. That was partly at the root of my own drinking; the freedom to express my feelings was repressed and drinking became the "medicine" to help me.

However, AA is set up and designed to produce compliant individuals who will have an unquestioning "respect" for hierarchy (it is an unhealthy respect, not a true one in which the individual can question the authority). Anger is considered a very "tricky" element and the "groupthink" does its utmost to discourage it by shaming and blaming.

During my time in AA, I often censored my sharing or my conversations to exclude my "angry stuff". This was dangerous for me and definitely stunted my personal growth. This neglect to accept anger in AA results in anger directed inward, inducing low self-esteem and anxiety.

Punitive phrases and harsh sponsors bordering on the sadistic are commonplace in AA. I still get angry when I think about that as it is still going on every day in thousands of meetings across the world. One of the reasons why I am writing this, is to add to the growing number of books and papers that are revealing the dark side of AA.

10. "I was loved into wellness- I found myself where I needed to be, not where I chose to be"

A frightening admission I heard from a woman with 33 years "sobriety". How did that happen? I wanted to say; "if you were that vulnerable all those years ago, haven't you seriously questioned that since then?" But I said nothing. I think this clearly shows the continuing self-deceit that is a huge part of AA brainwashing, the word that I know all good AA members will rage at; (quietly, in a repressed, passive-aggressive sort of way).

The Oxford dictionary definition of brainwashing is as follows;

"To implant ideas, especially ideology into a person/s by repetition".

> There is no good or bad brainwashing; there is just brainwashing and AA bases its programme on it.
>
> Self-reflection is the marker of a healthy person. The "old-timer" I quote from had done no such reflection beyond a Step 4 and 5, and a daily "maintenance" step 10). Let me translate; step 4; made a searching and fearless moral inventory of ourselves (guilty search for character defects which all human beings share,) then a step 5; admitted to God, to ourselves, and to another human being the exact nature of our wrongs (a full-on religious confessional step.
>
> In AA you are required to tell God first (if you believe in him), then yourself; then confess to someone else (usually a peer in AA who has no qualifications other than being a person who also misuses drink/drugs as you have done) Look at step 10;

"Step 10; continued to take personal inventory and when we were wrong promptly admitted it."

(This confessional carousel never ends and you are encouraged, daily to look at everything that is wrong with you/your behaviour)

The onus is on the confessor, as a flawed, defective human being, to miserably recount their sins to another on a regular basis – this specifically emulates religious structures and destroys once and for all the myth that AA is not a religious programme. This is not self-reflection; this is self-flagellation and is the cornerstone of the fellowship programme.

If a health professional is reading this, you need to know that this is what happens each day within the anonymous programme of AA. Now place in your mind a severely damaged victim of familial sexual abuse over decades. This is the programme that fragile person will be following; with no outside regulation, no accountability. If that isn't a sobering thought, I don't know what is.

Outpourings such as AA encourage (as in all creeds and religions) usually only result in temporary relief, resulting in the perpetual returning of the "sinner" when he/she/they have committed offence against "god" or another person. Unless there is a qualified professional following a plan tailored to the individual and their issues, there will be no long-lasting insights or self-awareness and self-acceptance – the aim of good mental health in someone who has experienced trauma and consequent drink/drug misuse.

AA has sponsors, and is not designed for someone to get well and to leave the group. Once you have joined, you have joined for life and your mission is to recruit.

You cannot be "loved into wellness" in such a fashion. This is a trite, insulting phrase, particularly for anyone from an abusive background. It can easily be hijacked by predatory group members (of any sex) to manipulate vulnerable newcomers (of any age).

11. "What was your part in it?"

On the face of it, that question seems like it could be reflective and helpful – if it is taken in context with qualified professional guidance. In AA, it can, and often is, turned into a tool for self-blame and recrimination. It also gives predators a green light.

Apologists for abusive behaviour abound in AA, under the cloak of "forgiveness". One of my biggest criticisms of the 4th & 5th step process (inventory and confession) is that very often vulnerable people either self-disclose far too quickly with an unsuitable person (and they cannot cope with the can of worms they have unleashed) or they clam up, write and confess a false account that they think will get them through, thereby repressing the massive changes they are going through with no real awareness or safeguarding in place.

They tick the box. The person who has "overshared" very often goes "back out" to use alcohol/drugs again and becomes a "relapser". They are considered to have failed and on return must repeat the whole process again. Remember, there are no checks and balances in AA. Only peers.

In a way, I was fortunate to complete my steps 4 & 5 in a treatment centre. I was, in some part, "held" in a fairly safe environment (but not safe by any real definition of the word!) I dutifully wrote and read my list of woes and questionable behaviours to a complete stranger, an older woman who I had never met before and never saw again after that day. I think the treatment centre bussed them in from other locales; "rent-a-confessor" or some such organisation….

I felt completely drained after my confession and was allowed to go to my dorm room and take a nap – something never usually allowed in the normal day to day routine of the centre.

This was a special occasion. Much is made of this prostration before God process and the "relief" it brings. It makes me feel quite sick when I recall it.

Returning to the slogan "what was your part in it?", if I apply that to my step 4/5 experience at the treatment centre, my part was not asking who the hell the person was who I was "confessing my wrongdoings" to and also for writing an enormous essay about my life that became the "case for the prosecution" in my head.

It gave my inner critic total permission to class me as defective, weak, unable to make good choices or be self-reliant and it actively harmed my fragile sense of self. This process is the "breaking down" formula, very similar to that used in military training establishments. It leaves one empty and dependent, yearning for stability and structure.

However, I did survive treatment with a big chunk of my inner self intact. Steps 4 & 5 are at the crux of AA damage. I'm now ok with "my part in it". My part is to help reveal the bad practice, unregulated power and dangerous brainwashing that suspends one's critical thinking. This continues on in the outmoded institution of AA, beloved by media and celebrity culture alike.

12. "A Day at a time"

Perhaps the best known and most used of all AA slogans – now in common usage and the foundation of AA recovery. In my early days in AA, I had so much practical "mess" in my life and I needed practical help. My confidence and ability to seek the help I needed was at a low point.

In essence, "a day at a time" seems very helpful; a way to allay future anxieties, it's a way to "keep it simple" (AA slogan).

What was happening for me was that I would attend 2 or even 3 meetings a day and find I had actually achieved no further practical steps to get my life back on track (that's when I went to the doctor to ask for therapy). AA would say, "ah, but you have stayed sober today" as if this was the only achievement that mattered. Yes, of course it did, but it really wasn't everything. (I never said that out loud).

What with meetings and coffee meet ups and steps and reading AA literature, I seemed to have no agency in the day to day running of my life after treatment.

This went on for about 6 months, then I took a decision to go to less meetings, my relationship with Derek was on the rocks too and I didn't want to bump into him every five minutes. I began to plan my escape. I applied to college as a mature student, got a grant and left Bristol to live in Bath and take a performing arts course, something I had originally applied for at the start of my sober life – I had been dissuaded by my 13th stepping boyfriend….

Now I had a stronger resolve and some helpful therapy under my belt. It was a good move, one that began to disentangle me from the cloying, claustrophobic AA network that felt like mistletoe around my neck at times. What had started out as a "new beginning" now looked very much like servitude to me.

I had become enmeshed in the AA world "a day at a time"! This is how brainwashing works. Something initially appealing or offering some relief becomes a habitual dependence (just like alcohol/drugs) and doesn't want to let you go. The best you can hope for is "Stockholm syndrome" where you empathize with the hostage takers. But you are still a hostage.

In my new location and firmly established on a course I loved, I became involved in Codependents Anonymous, another branch of the 12-step family tree. It felt slightly kinder, but it had as many faults and drawbacks as AA. Even at that early stage, I was looking for ways to disengage with 12 step life; CODA seemed the soft exit drug compared with the harsh smack of AA.

My college days were full, challenging and great fun; most of the students were 10 years younger than me and I felt like I was reliving a youth I never had – it was very healing in so many ways and I came away with a distinction in the course modules; drama, language of theatre, music, singing, dance and stagecraft – it was fantastic. I felt like "me" again and I refrained from any intimate relationships, wanting no distractions from my focus on the course. I was getting well, I didn't want to drink, I was coping with new responsibilities, making mistakes, picking myself up and enjoying life again.

If I have any regrets in my life (and I have very few) I would like to have stopped all fellowship groups at that point. That is the truth with the benefit of hindsight of course! My brainwashing (mainly due to the intense 11-week treatment centre programme) was ingrained and I really believed that I could not live properly without some connection with AA or another 12-step fellowship programme. I was still hooked.

I also think that had I been aware of other recovery/treatment programmes, I would have explored them. Choice is the key and one which is sadly lacking in the treatment of alcohol/drug issues. This is changing rapidly, I believe and if I was at the same point now, I definitely would be looking anywhere else other than AA.

AA never promotes "outside help" and discourages experimentation with other organisations, even religious ones. I've heard Buddhists castigated in open meetings for "confusing their recovery with other commitments".

"A day at a time" seems innocuous and a positive phrase for people who have no structure or hope in their lives. It is a vacuous one. I would replace it now with "each day I find the strength to do some stuff, some days it's great, other days I don't do much, and that's ok"

AA living means a full-time, unpaid (unless you are at the top of the AA Charity and get a nice big salary), life-long commitment to something that ultimately does nothing concrete for you. My day is my business nowadays.

13. Keep coming back, it works if you work it"

There is, literally, no end to your bondage to this organisation. What little time you have left after going to meetings, sponsoring, making a living, going out with AA members for coffee over interminable discussions about sobriety and fellowship matters must be spent in SERVICE. Phone duty (though you are not a trained professional primed for first responding calls from traumatized people), 12 step interventions at hospital/home bedsides (again you are very likely not trained in trauma intervention, but AA doesn't worry about that), chairing a group, making coffee/tea, literature secretary, treasurer, meet and greeter……. the list goes on.

Forget your own desires and needs – AA comes first. I have heard many hundreds of people say "AA comes before my family, my children, my job. My sobriety must come first"

The rationale is that without AA, you are nothing. AA supports enthusiastically the disease model of alcoholism. I do not. I do believe alcohol and drug misuse affect people in different ways but I do not believe it is transferred genetically or that alcoholics/addicts are in some way different from other people.

There is plenty of evidence now that disproves the disease theory which was initially based on a small percentage of (mainly male) alcoholics and is totally outdated. AA, because of its planned model of financially viable treatment centres, was quick to cleave to this disease led approach, yet the 12 step programmes do not have anything scientific at their core. 12 suggested steps, inventory, confession and prayers……….and KEEP COMING BACK, IT WORKS IF YOU WORK IT!" It isn't enough, by a very long chalk.

AA is truly the candy floss of programmes for living. Before you know it, your life will be over. I thought about that a lot when I was having intensive chemotherapy for Stage 4 cancer, followed by a stem cell transplant in 2019. I decided then that I didn't want to be on my deathbed thinking "why did I go to so many AA meetings?"

Cancer intensified my focus on what was important, and I realised that AA wasn't. However, I still went to meetings for some of 2021 when Lockdown came into force. Throughout my cancer, AA was noticeably "not there". Three people stayed in touch, one who I clicked with would have been a friend anyway.

"It works if you work it" is the Protestant work ethic at its most toxic. If it doesn't work it means you are lazy, unable to grasp this wonderful programme that has "saved the lives of thousands" (we don't hear about the thousands who relapse, many who die and we also don't hear about the many suicides of desperate people who do not get pointed to real, practical help when they need it, AA takes absolutely no responsibility for that) Don't forget that it is a registered charity that receives thousands in individual donations each year.

Treatment centres do not come cheap and many people, and their families are bankrupted as they plough cash into yet another treatment regime. It's not uncommon for people to enter treatment 5,6,7,8 times! No wonder they call it the swing door of sobriety.

Or maybe you are one of the unfortunates -the "constitutionally incapable" as the Big Book says, of adhering to "this simple programme" ….

What works is YOU, YOU as a person in your own right finding rewarding new ways to act, respond, live and work in society.

You do that by your own hand and you are not powerless over alcohol. Total rubbish. Certainly, we get help along the way, but it is not help with an obligation "to serve" in return. AA does not make you sober, not does it keep you sober. You do.

Our thinking changes prior to taking a drink or drug and can be regulated, as most thinking patterns can (with specialized help in trauma-based usage). I drank for a variety of reasons; fear, anxiety, sadness, grief, anger, depression, loneliness, lack of work, all those issues needed addressing once I'd given up drinking. Drinking didn't help, I knew that unequivocally before I'd even discovered AA. That's why I stopped. On my own.

The "affliction" mentioned in AA literature (a very archaic word) can be cured and/or managed. Many people go back to drinking in a way that does not disrupt their or others' lives. There is a wealth of scientific evidence and ongoing research on addiction and moderation of usage.

People with severe mental health issues are given "starter" literature in AA which is infantile and simplistic and can further plunge the "newcomer" into depression and ill-health as their serious, underlying issues are left neglected. Just pray and hand it over.

I read the Big Book in treatment (it was a requirement; I was on a Hazelden 12 step programme) and over the years I have sat in meetings and read out sections of the book; though I avoided "Big Book" meetings if at all possible.

With a few minor additions and alterations, it still stands as the foundation book for alcoholics in 12 step programmes.

Bill W is the revered and oft-quoted writer. There is plenty of information online about him. He was a flawed man who was in the right place at a particular time in post-prohibition America. And he milked it. AA is still milking it.

I asked myself many times over the years, "do I want to base my best chances of a decent life on the ramblings of a philandering ex-salesman who asks me to get on my knees and pray and hand over my power to something I don't believe in?"

It took me years to eventually get out completely and to come to this point in my life where I want a very bright torch to be shone onto this religious organisation that wields so much power in the health professions, media, showbusiness and the corridors of government, and holds a lot of money in its coffers. Whether or not you believe AA to be a helpful, altruistic organisation, or an old-fashioned con game, as I do, I think at the very least, an independent body needs to regulate its operations. AA is comprised of vulnerable, damaged people in various stages of wellness. They deserve, at the very minimum, safety in "the rooms".

Ordinary people are being deceived in AA every day. As "users", we all deserve better treatment packages and ongoing support. It's far too easy for courts and health professionals to send people to AA and NA when they know little or nothing about how these programmes work. It really is time for change.

Chapter 3

The 13th Step

AA has 12 steps to its programme, but there is an unofficial step, one that is not written down but is acknowledged by members as a persistent "hidden" problem.

"13th stepping" a newcomer (of any age/gender) means influencing or manipulating a vulnerable person, usually sexually but it can also be financially and psychologically. Someone with a measure of "sober time" basically preys on the newcomer, using influence and power inappropiately

In my own experience, men practice this step in greater numbers than women, but it is rife across genders. I was 13th stepped; many of the women I knew in AA also were. I began seeking out women only or gay/lesbian groups when I found some mixed groups to be so toxic, that to go there would be a form of punishment for me and often put my "recovery" back by weeks.

To put it bluntly, there are a lot of serial shaggers and sexually manipulative people in AA, and it doesn't get addressed or called out often, due to the closed nature and protection of the "anonymous" part of AA. In light of so much exposure these days in the media, I think there's a good case for renaming AA, "Alcoholics Ubiquitous".

Maybe readers will consider I am being naïve expecting people to regulate themselves in a mixed group of damaged, vulnerable people; however, I would call your attention to the fact that AA is a registered charity with its head office employees earning 6 figure incomes.

It is frequently held up as the only model of getting and staying sober, a claim that has been rarely challenged by a society that is quick to delegate all responsibility for huge alcohol/drug misuse problems to an organisation who says it has the magic pill; "thankyou AA, now we don't have to think about this anymore"

Courts order mandatory attendance as part of sentencing; in the US particularly, but also increasingly in the UK. (I have no knowledge of what happens in other judicial systems around the world, but AA is a worldwide organisation). Treatment centres are not free, they are a massive money-making merry-go-round for the companies who own them.

Why does AA not come under more scrutiny for the behaviours and actions of its members? Tradition 4 states that "each group should be autonomous except in matters affecting other groups, or AA as a whole". This tradition would be the ideal starting point for discussion/regulation and change in respect of sexual misconduct/abuse within the fellowship groups. You would think so, wouldn't you? Except that it isn't.

When the GSR (group service representative; each group has one) reports back to Inter-group (the meeting of local groups to monitor issues arising from each individual group) there is often the response "we cannot interfere with an individual group, you must hold a Group Conscience meeting to resolve this".

In other words; "no way are we dealing with this hot potato! You decide what to do, but don't forget that you can't compromise someone's anonymity" This is the Klingon Shielding device that keeps predators safe from police intervention. A "group conscience" meeting, by the way, is called whenever an individual group wants to discuss changes in the meeting; e.g., Start time, vacant posts needing to be filled, points of order regarding readings/prayers used etc.

In my experience they are usually controlled by a few staunch "old-timers" in the meeting and rarely do real issues ever get raised or dealt with. The "toxic minority" (as I call them) get to call the shots. To bring up a sexual misconduct incident will bring the acid rain of shame upon your head. Thus the 13th stepper continues on unimpeded.

It's the perpetual "closed shop" system in operation, but I see many more people coming out with stories on YouTube and other forums, and I believe the next 5 years will see a sea-change in getting abusers brought to public awareness.

Monica Richardson, who was a long-time AA member for over 30 years in the USA made a film called "The 13th Step in 2016; a critical and timely expose of AA, resulting in many women coming forward, eager to be heard for the first time. AA is not a safe haven for many people. Monica continues to work in groups and blogs, raising awareness of AA misconduct throughout its structure.

In all the mixed groups I attended, without exception, there were predators. Certain men get a reputation for hugging too close and too often, some women will kiss and be best friends with a newcomer or offer financial assistance or a place to stay, with their own sexual agenda firmly in their minds.

Coffee and a chat after the meeting can turn into a minefield of sexual overtones, or inappropriate sharing of past experiences, or "jokes" that are not jokes at all, but are intended to make newcomers feel uncomfortable, thereby increasing the power hold of the "old timer".

It stinks like 3-day old fish and it is commonplace. I always kept an eye on young female newcomers as best I could – yet I feel bad sometimes that I didn't do more, that I didn't raise my concerns with the GSR or intergroup, though I did write a letter when the Intergroup tried to make one of our all women groups into a mixed group.

We had all agreed that it made us feel safer because of the sensitivity of the experiences we were sharing, some for the first time in our lives. The letter was sent to "conference" and we got to keep our group as we wanted it. However, most groups stay in the control of the "toxic minority" and no changes are encouraged or discussed. The dysfunctional "family" gets to keep its nasty secrets in the cupboard and the members stay in line, back into lockstep with the "programme".

At a meeting I regularly attended, a guy who I knew as an acquaintance, came into the kitchen, picked me up by my middle and swung me around, saying I had a lovely smile. I was furious and almost punched him. He became angry because I had not seen his actions as "fun", and he angrily shouted that he was being affectionate.

This sort of crap goes on daily in AA. Poor boundaries, lack of a proper complaints procedure (and safeguarding) and the famous lack of accountability of AA combine to make many meetings very unsafe.

Yet there is lip service paid frequently to the "rule" that men give their numbers to men and women give their numbers to men, in the hope that this will avoid any inappropriate fraternizing or abuse of power. Loose guidelines for a flabby set-up and an even flabbier outcome – and a dangerous one in many cases.

Treatment centres constantly re-iterate the "no fraternizing or you are out" rule. While I was in treatment for 11 weeks, quite a few people were made to leave as their libidos returned, full-steam ahead.

The more I reflect on inappropriate sexual behaviours and harassment in AA, the more anger I connect with about the times I either witnessed it or was on the receiving end of it. I don't believe the general public or the fawning media have any idea what "treatment" is like (though TV/Hollywood spends big dollars on portraying the establishments in a growing spate of shows).

AA and its history are so embedded now in our culture as a benign force for good that it is hard to challenge that as an individual who has lived through it. Though I think that is changing as more of us band together to share our experiences of being in, then out of fellowship programmes.

Literally thousands of people are leaving AA or trying out other frameworks for recovery; e.g., SMART, harm reduction, the Sinclair method, women alcoholics in recovery – there are a fast-growing collection of modules and groups.

Temperance is chic and makes money, that's for certain, but for myself I avoid programmes or one particular method. I don't want to drink anymore, it's really as simple as that for me. With ongoing therapy, friends, creative projects and family commitments I do it my own way. I don't believe in god. The closest I come to spirituality is the awe I experience in the natural world and the goodness of many people I have met along the way.

The USA are ahead of us in the UK in their rejection of programme methods of treatment; the avalanche there is spreading to the UK, in no small part due to Covid era zoom meetings (tuning in to meetings all over the world and also seeing bullshit multiplied across the globe!)

There's a #metoo effect taking place, one I am very glad is happening if it means closer examination of a structure that is not accountable to the public and in which many people feel controlled, dismissed or simply confused with outdated methods of dealing with alcohol/drug misuse. I haven't even mentioned the systemic bullying by sponsors yet….

The horror stories will keep coming until the media will have to rub the stardust of AA myths and fables from their eyes and see the truth; AA is not a safe place for vulnerable people. It reinforces stereotypes, is misogynistic, (it still remains unaccountable in dealing with many sexual harassment and rape crimes; even when they are reported via AA's group structures which monitor group proceedings; of course, they are rarely reported due to the shame of those victims and because their sponsors usually tell them to look at "their part" in the incident, thereby planting the blame firmly back with the victim)

This may sound shocking; it is. I also want to highlight the fact that many small incidents of sexually inappropriate behaviour often go unmissed, unremarked upon as they are accepted by the group. To even bring up the subject of sexually inappropriate behaviour of a group member will often result in being ostracized.

Don't just take my word for it; read the stories of many, many women and men who have relapsed or left AA because of these reasons. I've lost count of the thousands of times I've been addressed as "sweetheart", "darling", "girl" by middle-aged men – even when I've been years older than them. The whole atmosphere is one of immaturity and false closeness, masked as "humour" and friendship.

Historically, women were not allowed to join AA – it was thought they could not be alcoholics. That changed, of course, but initially AA was a middle-class boys club. The fake equality that pervades "the rooms" does nothing for the self-esteem of thousands of vulnerable women particularly, who are looking for solutions to help them deal with complex problems, including drinking too much.

One-size does not fit all. I do not mention trans-people here simply because back in the 80's I did not know any in the fellowships. I did know trans people in the world of performance, but I do not have the experience from my AA "world" to include any observations here.

Again, this inclines me to think that "difference" is not particularly welcomed in AA. However, I am sure if there are Trans AA groups, they will be no less subject to the brainwashing and cod-spirituality experienced by anyone.

The 13th step persists because there is no change in AA attitudes, because it resists all challenges to its structure and traditions. It is a registered charity with employees earning healthy salaries at its World Service Incorporated headquarters

. Public accountability and the safeguarding of its millions of members need to be at the top of the list for those working in journalism and media. AA members who are deprogramming are one of the pressure groups that collectively will push for this change. This should be welcomed, particularly amongst the many millions of communities struggling with alcohol and drug misuse; lives cut short for lack of proper care and treatment.

Chapter 4

In Treatment

"Hazelden began in 1949, with the revolutionary idea of creating a humane, therapeutic community for alcoholics and addicts. Once this idea was ridiculed, today it is seen as commonplace." (from the Hazelden Betty Ford webpage)

My "treatment" was the Hazelden, "Minnesota model" (in use at the famous Betty Ford clinic in the USA at the time I went into treatment in the UK in the late 80's),using the 12-step programme of Alcoholics Anonymous. It consisted of 8 weeks primary care in "the big house", followed by 4 weeks secondary care where groups of 4-5 people shared houses in a small satellite facility 100 yards from the main house.

In secondary care, each housemate had chores and were expected to submit a diary each week to their counsellor, outlining their activities (which had to include at least 5 AA/NA meetings). I left secondary care after 2 weeks – actually I was kicked out because I wouldn't fill in the diary to their satisfaction and because my counsellor said I was not "showing commitment". I couldn't wait to go.

Let's return to primary care. I went into the centre 6 months sober or "dry" as they liked to describe it. I'd been to some meetings, but this progression to treatment was basically "sold" to me by my 13th stepping boyfriend (who had attended the same treatment centre 3 years previously). I was vulnerable and suggestible. I went along with the idea, thinking that he was only looking out for my best interests.

In later years, long after we had split up, he suffered continued mental breakdowns and I believe his "treatment" at the centre completely missed all the signs of severe mental health problems. He'd also attended Al-a teen (a 12-step fellowship programme for young people, so he was indoctrinated early on in his life).

These would have been picked up by a qualified health professional, instead of him being given a 12-step programme and the choice to pray and "let go, let God".

I slept in a dormitory with 5 other women. We weren't allowed to stay in the dorm during the day and there was a strict regime for mealtimes and group therapy (twice a day). Also, after the first week, we were given chores around the house. Everyone was at a different stage of the treatment programme as there was a rolling intake of people.

Some people went straight into de-tox as they had come in drunk/using and needed medication to control the effects of coming off substances. We had the variety pack of allcomers; alcoholics, addicts, gamblers, glue sniffers, pill poppers, over-eaters, anorexics and even some co-dependents who were considered the lowest in the hierarchy (and there definitely was one).

The heroin addicts usually congregated around the gas fire and were eternally miserable and considered themselves the only "true addicts" in the place. When I recall it now, it was like a Nightmare Camp of Broken people with no one in charge. I never felt safe the entire time I was there.

We had "group" twice a day with 2 counsellors sitting in at each group of about 10 people. As I said before, it was a "rolling programme" of treatment, so you would find yourself with day-old newcomers to the centre as well as 8-weekers about to graduate to secondary care.

This model of recovery mixes up the "addicts" in order to challenge each person at every stage of their process. I really had no idea what was going on some times and it's taken me years of reading and professional therapy to assess what was actually going on.

At every group, counsellors would "bait" someone who was showing signs of "denial" and encourage other group members to call the person out on something they had "lied" about. I've been on the receiving end of that ploy many times and it is shaming, cruel and useless as a way to make someone aware of their behaviour. Here I will quote information from the Hazelden Betty Ford Foundation, available to all on the internet;

"Alcoholism is a disease. Attempts to chide, shame or scold an alcoholic into abstinence are essentially useless. Instead, we can view alcoholism as an involuntary disability – a disease – and treat it as such"

Apparently, it is ok to "chide and shame" an "alcoholic when it suits the counsellors. Was my cancer an "involuntary disability"? Is alcoholism comparable? How did they set the bar here; from a background of "clinical experience" or so it says on the webpage.

Like everyone else there (without exception), I developed coping mechanisms (or rather I used the ones I had learned in my family of origin) to give the impression that I was "getting the programme".

Quite a few people just upped and left whilst I was there. There are no locks on the doors, everyone goes in of their own accord and can leave at any time…. they are then condemned to "go back out there and try one more drink and see if you can handle it". I heard a counsellor say that as a middle-aged man packed his bags and headed for the nearest pub (the one nearest the centre did a roaring trade with escapees).

I was given AA approved literature to read. (Remember too that these were the "olden days"; no mobiles, no lap-tops, just an old TV we could watch in the evenings and a pay-phone in the hall that meant a long queue every night to get the chance to talk to the "outside world").

I am an avid reader and it was one of the few opportunities) when I could switch off from everything going on around me. I read "Love is letting go of fear" (Gerald G. Jampolsky MD, still in print) which I thought was ok, though a bit sentimental in its overall message; "The Road Less travelled" (M. Scott Peck, which everyone read at the time, and a book on anger because a female counsellor told me I was the angriest person in the centre! What a great way to build trust……. not really!

In some ways, I rambled through it like a strange dream. I met some very interesting people who had lived amazing lives; I met people who had done nothing other than drink/use drugs since childhood; others had started late in life. It was a motley crew and no mistake. There were some very unpleasant crew members too who I did my utmost to avoid. I heard some horrendous war stories from some very damaged men – one told me he had killed two people and that he'd never told anyone before…. I don't even know if this was true or simply bravado, but I do know it was totally inappropriate and it added to my feelings of acute insecurity in the place.

Several men made sexual advances to me and there were also many men unable to deal with very toxic anger in themselves, leaving most of the women feeling very vulnerable around them. I didn't report any of it to the counsellors; I thought it was all part of the "mix" of treatment and I had poor boundaries and low self-esteem.

We all got very close, very quickly. I regularly heard women sharing intimate details of familial sexual abuse, incest and multiple rapes. It was something that I had never experienced before. I believe I was mentally scarred in the wake of this continual disclosure as I too was damaged and vulnerable and had no "filters" to make sense of what I was hearing.

Also, the disclosures often left the women feeling very drained and insecure, particularly if they had never accessed any of the memories before. It felt wrong; too much openness with no real support. The back-up for these incredibly painful life experiences was the 12 step AA programme; powerlessness, handing our will over to god, confession, inventory of self and prayer.

All the counsellors were recovering alcoholics/addicts and each had their own "style" of approaching the treatment regime. I was fortunate in some respects because my counsellor was a man who had been bullied mercilessly for his entire young life and he was a very sensitive soul, I instinctively felt I could trust him. I didn't really trust any of the other counsellors.

However, I was only allotted one face to face session with him per week; on reflection this seems utterly ridiculous. The rest of the time I had to try and resolve my "issues" in "group therapy" which felt like being thrown to the wolves twice daily, then having to show gratitude for it.

Free time was sometimes even more threatening for me. That was when most of the inappropriate sexual advances, innuendoes and grooming took place. I used to dread evenings from about 6-10pm when everyone gathered in the smoke-filled lounge. It was worse than any pub or bar that I ever went into.

I got close to some women and a few men but I still felt unsafe, perpetually hypervigiliant. This type of treatment was completely unsuited to my particular character. My self-esteem was slowly but surely eroded in that centre and it did nothing to address any of the real issues I was facing in my life in preparation for going "back out into the real world"

I felt that I was being encouraged daily to betray my inner core self just to belong, to show I was "on the programme". I had to be willing to compromise my very essence so that I could be a "grateful, recovering alcoholic". It was terrible, but I stayed, stuck it out with my usual tenacity. If there's one thing I learned in my family, it was how to survive –

but it came at a price, and I was reliving those feelings daily with no safety net.

I managed the whole 8 weeks of primary care (it seemed much longer), got my "medallion" and transferred to secondary care. I don't know how people survive boarding school; there were quite a few ex-boarders in the centre; many found treatment painfully familiar, particularly those who had experienced abuse by staff members at their former schools.

I stayed because I was keen to please – and to keep – my AA boyfriend. Simple as that. But I think the reward came at a high mental cost to me. With hindsight, I am still shocked at the casual, unprofessional handling of all those damaged people (me included) in close proximity for at least 8 weeks.

Getting through "primary" is a big milestone in treatment centres. Back then, we went through a ritual where the counsellor hands you your "medallion" of success and then the whole community in the centre gathers in a circle and one by one literally "lovebombs" you, telling anecdotes of how you have made such huge progress since you came "through the doors" and how amazing you are going to be once you get back out into society and "carry the message" of AA.

I felt physically and mentally very strange afterwards. "Unreal and out of it" is the nearest description I can give. Of course, now I know that I was exhibiting dissociative behaviour; I was disoriented from myself, a familiar childhood state for me.

When I had read my" Step 4" (my searching and fearless moral inventory) to a complete stranger at the centre, I'd gone to sleep immediately afterwards and felt empty; unpleasantly so, as if I had been unpicked and not put back together.

These experiences were largely unmonitored as far as I could tell. No meaningful assessment of "inmates" was apparent as we went through these "mind-stripping" steps on the "road to recovery". There weren't enough staff to do that; and there certainly weren't enough specially trained/qualified staff members to respond to the many different issues that each person was dealing with.

I packed my bag, had my last meal in the dining room where I felt suddenly very detached from the other inmates. I walked the short distance through the gardens to the secondary care complex, but it felt like another world – one that I didn't really want to be in.

I shared a room with a woman called Winnie, a Scots woman who I got on ok with, but who was also so full of undealt with rage that it was like waiting for a grenade pin to be pulled. She put on a front of peace-loving hippy child of the Universe but when she told me her story of terrible abuse and family violence, I knew she needed more than prayers and a primary care medallion.

I often wonder what happened to her, how her life panned out after treatment. When I left the facility, I exchanged numbers with quite a few people and did keep in touch with some for a while. There were people from America, the UK, Jersey, Portugal, France and Spain.

The centre had a long waiting list, with both private and NHS patients (this was often a cause for argument in the lounge, with the private patients feeling hard-done-by because those on the NHS were getting treatment "for free"). Actually, AA receives that NHS funding, so who benefits the most? AA, of course.

After a year, those connections dwindled to one, then to none and I felt odd that I didn't really feel any connection, despite all the trauma and time we had spent in the centre together. For me, this reflects on how dissociated I was from my actual experience there. It felt like a "false" experience rather than an authentic one.

Some probably died, some went back to drinking/using and some remained abstinent, like me. Many may have gone to AA but also, it's likely that a lot did not. Statistics for "recovery" following treatment are not readily available and AA is notoriously shy about giving hard evidence of its success rates in these 12 step centres. I imagine they are poor. I cannot see that the "treatment" given to me and the rest of my fellows at the centre could give long-lasting, effective healing. No way.

I needed a lot of one-to-one therapy to get over my treatment experience and I'm sure many others did too. If what I describe is still going on in the UK with the same patterns and methods of treatment, then I don't feel we have come very far as a society in dealing with the huge alcohol/drug misuse issues we have.

There is a growing community of people wanting multiple paths to recovery; in fact, there is a group called exactly that and they have conferences each year to share best practice. (In the USA, not sure if UK has any yet).

One of the memories from treatment that has just flashed up for me was particularly harsh and shaming.

As a musician/performer I entered treatment with none of my usual distractions, but I still liked to dress up each day in fairly flamboyant clothes, simply because it was one of the few things I could do to cheer myself up in that shitty place.

One morning I got to group at 10 am for the session and my least favourite counsellor, Sue was in "the chair" ready to roast us. Every time she had the whip hand, she reduced women to tears and men to blind, red rage. In me, she induced a sort of frozenness. I would try and become like a curtain that was drawn and harmless. It never worked. Her killer instincts were switched on and she wasted no opportunity if there was someone "hiding", whom she could "unpick".

I was wearing a floppy cerise cardigan (very 80's), tight black skinny jeans and monkey boots. I thought I looked cool. 20 minutes went by as Sue focused on a two-days-in newcomer. She was still raw and wondering where she was. I stayed silent while Sue encouraged the group to give the "newbie" a grilling. The poor girl (only 18) was close to breaking, I could tell, and I knew the tears were forthcoming.

And just then I shifted my position and made an involuntary humming noise, a default behaviour I often resorted to in my family home when I sensed an approaching bust-up between my parents or my sister and myself. Sue swung round, laser-like suddenly aware of my discomfort (just as my parents had been) The focus was now on me….

"Marilyn, you seem distracted today? Do you have any input that could help?" I felt hot and flushed and immediately wanted to get up and leave. "Not really", I offered, weakly. "I'm not sure you're really with us Marilyn" she began, and I sensed the groups interest in my predicament.

Sue went on; "You come in every day in a different multi-coloured outfit – sometimes like a bag-lady, sometimes like a model; which are you? Who are you trying to impress? Do we really know who you are?" She went on in this vein for a long time (probably 10 minutes at most, it felt like much longer)

Long enough for me to feel so low about myself that I just couldn't respond. I didn't cry, I didn't show anger; I felt completely and utterly deflated. Then she returned to her original baiting of the newcomer and ignored me for the remainder of the session. I've never forgotten it. There was no "follow-up" to what had happened and I think it was probably my "rock-bottom" in primary treatment. How can this practice of "tough love" be considered helpful or useful?

Who was monitoring the counsellor's behaviour? Who was aware of what was going on? Each counsellor seemed to have arbitrary control over their own groups and they definitely had "favourites" amongst us alcoholics/addicts. I don't even know if they undertook "supervision" sessions such as trained accredited therapists get on a regular basis.

I realise now how little I knew about the organisation and its staff, and how trustingly I had given over my power and well-being to them when I was at a low ebb in my life.

That, in essence, is how a cult operates. It is a "sealed society"; it offers help and support if you agree to the conditioning ("this simple programme"). In the process, it destroys your identity and replaces it with a programme of thinking that you must strictly adhere to, in order to stay "sane and well".

2 weeks into secondary care I rang my Dad and he came and collected me, he had thought from the start that it was all snake-oil and fakery. I got out through non-compliance, but the damage I had gone into treatment with was now compounded with a massive dose of shame and a fear of what lay ahead for me as a non-drinker on the "outside". This should not be the outcome of "treatment".

Chapter 5

You have a disease

There is a very seductive subtext to this statement. Many people believe it to be absolutely true, largely due to the fact that AA has continually flooded the media and health institutions with the "disease model" of alcoholism/addiction. They did invent it after all, with some amicable scientists enlisted to verify the theory.

No actual evidence exists to link genetic codes or markers to "alcoholism". Heavy drinking usage and drug taking in families does tend to be generational; but learned behaviours and trauma have a huge impact on an individual's coping mechanisms and often lead to addiction problems. Alcohol was my coping mechanism and also, eventually, my problem.

I was told, in the treatment centre, that alcoholism was a disease and I had it. The Doctor, in my intake interview, showed me the "disease curve" of alcoholism, which has been used for decades (Dr Jelinek's curve) and he told me I was a "chronic alcoholic". I was 30, and I had drunk heavily, off and on since the age of 15.

Drinking had definitely got me into difficult and dangerous situations. I was breathalyzed for drink/driving. Somehow, I evaded prosecution; I think my enlarged singers' lungs helped me on that score; I'm not boasting because I have no idea how I got off that charge. Drinking had lost me jobs; relationships and I also had a miscarriage (it later transpired that I had "spontaneously miscarried" due to an incompatibility of blood groups between myself and my partner, it had nothing to do with alcohol) just before I decided to give up drinking. It was a wake-up call; it was one of many. However, I do not believe I was ever an "alcoholic". I used drink to cover emotional pain and to switch off when I felt the world was too overwhelming, which it often was to me.

Yet, I also I had a lot of fun with drinking; lots of events in London when I worked in Public Relations were flowing with drink, and it wasn't all miserable! My music and theatrical projects abounded with drinking buddies and parties. I wasn't always crashing through a window or lying in a gutter (commonly told tales at AA meetings, few of which I believe these days). In no way do I intend here to dismiss the life-draining effects of drink and drugs on families and individuals; quite the reverse. Essentially, we need better help for anyone struggling to give up drink or drugs when they are ruining their lives.

Going back to my own story and my "disease", I remember I felt a sense of relief at having a label. Maybe, I thought, it would explain all the mental turmoil I had been through. It felt like a great big hook to hang everything on. I had a desperate desire for wellness and that, in itself is not the best foundation for lasting health. Desperation never is.

Also, I was in treatment, a "closed society" with everyone in the building telling me, every day that "alcoholism is a disease". On no occasion was I presented with any scientific evidence to prove this statement. In the absence of any other points of view or information (no google in those days!) it is easy to see how people, including myself came to believe this edict.

Science is not based on desperate hope or 12-step programmes that ask you to hand your will and your life over to a higher power. It uses experimentation and evidence on a continual quest to discover and present remedies, and sometimes cures for illnesses. It doesn't require faith to believe in it. It has controlled experimentation and results. And it is forever changing; someone new comes along to challenge the old theories and a new set of experiments begins……Such should it be with attitudes and models for "treatment programmes".

AA is not scientific; it is based on a religious programme of steps and traditions. It uses prayers and confession and god. When I had stage 4 cancer, I would have been appalled if my consultant haematologist had asked me to pray for my recovery and not to bother about the chemotherapy. Yet AA says that alcoholism is a disease, just like cancer! No, it is not, and that belief is insulting to people dealing with life-threatening illnesses.

I believe drinking is symptomatic of trauma issues, not the other way round. Whilst in treatment, I had a "family conference" where my parents were invited in to have a meeting with me and my counsellor. My Dad listened intently whilst my Mum was there under sufferance and didn't really seem to take any of it in (normal behaviour for her). At the end of it, my Dad took me aside and said" this is a load of rubbish Karen; what on earth are you doing in here?"

Many years later, I admitted to myself that he was right and it would have been a good move at that point to pack my bags and to leave with my parents. But I was in too deep and I was brainwashed by that time. I was also determined not to accept my parents help as I really needed to prove to myself that I could 'go it alone' and move forward in my life as a 'grown-up'.

When I had been "sober" for 15 years, my Dad said how proud he was of me and how I had turned my life around (he never gave AA any credit for it). He'd been a policeman for 30 years and could spot a scam a mile off.

At about this time, my husband had a heart attack (2 consecutive ones actually; he survived with stents and was very weakened for almost a year) Out of the woodwork came a disgruntled family member who sold our rented house from under us by auction, and there was also a possible diagnosis of leukemia on the horizon for our 7-year-old daughter.

To say my resilience and resources were stretched is a definite understatement. Fortunately, our daughter's illness proved to be a false alarm, but I felt sandbagged by it all. This all happened within a 2–4-month period. I felt so overwhelmed that I was propelled back to AA for some sort of stability and support (it was of very little help, and if anything, made me feel like taking a drink)

We moved to the Midlands and reset our lives, away from ties with AA for a long while; I got a job, our daughter went to school, we made new connections.

Fear, and specifically fear of death from the "disease of alcoholism" is the major draw that keeps you "coming back" to AA. I honestly believed I had alcoholism for life and never questioned that treatment centre doctor's, assessment of my "chronic" status. I changed this belief at a late stage of my time with AA. Partly because I was researching the internet much more and connecting with other "old timers" who had become disenchanted with fellowship programmes. Also, my perspective on life changed due to the cancer diagnosis I had in late 2018 when I went into a state of shock and my whole life was turned upside down. A critical event can alter everything, very fast and in that sense, I'm glad it did.

However, I have also become aware that there is a definite link between "new trauma/anxiety" and a compulsion to return to AA for me. My Dad was diagnosed with cancer in 2015 (he died 7 months after diagnosis) and I became estranged from my Mum and sister.

Everything about that time was painful, the most intense emotional pain that I had lived through. After a long absence, I went back to AA and also to CODA. Neither felt supportive or useful. None of the meetings felt like safe, holding places for all that I was going through, yet the hook was still there. The disconnect was huge. I compare it with a dysfunctional family that seems to offer solace but never comes up with the goods. It is redolent of the familiarity of abuse or neglect.

It was not a complete surprise when I was diagnosed with cancer myself, only 2 years after my fathers' death. The trauma of those years was contributory to my immune system taking a nosedive, and cancer got in through the back door.

Whilst going through cancer treatment, I broke off from AA. Three people from the fellowship stayed in touch and visited me or offered practical help. They were good people who I would have connected with anyway. Apart from that; nothing. AA is like a bubblegum-balloon, very pretty but fragile, liable to burst into a flat, sticky mess with no substance.

Yet even as I lay in my isolation room in hospital, I realised that after 34 years in AA, I didn't expect it to help me at all; I had never totally "bought the package". Whilst I had been working, raising a family, performing, writing, making new connections AA had slowly receded in importance. In fact, for 13 years of my "sobriety" I did no meetings whatsoever. And didn't drink or feel "less than" for not attending. I grew up.

2019 passed in a blur of intensive chemotherapy sessions and an autologous stem cell transplant to save my life. And then Covid hit the world. Post-cancer I developed shingles; a severe attack resulting in hospitalization and post-herpetic paralysis (which I still have). This was the last time I hopped back on to the AA bandwagon; onto zoom meetings in Lockdown.

I'd already been shielding at home for a year before most other people because of my compromised immune system. Now everyone was in Lockdown and AA meetings were no longer physical. I couldn't sing, do any music or writing (I was in a haze of pain medication at one point; that would constitute a "relapse" according to strict AA principles) and my daughter was looking after my physical needs while my husband continued working, from home. I felt lonely, frightened and without status or purpose; very common reactions in people recovering from serious, life-changing illness.

I went to meetings for a while on zoom, but never felt that they did me any good. My mind had cleared. I listened to the retelling of tales, the obedient references to a higher power, the "life is wonderful" platitudes….and I felt sick and flat. It was total bullshit. It always had been. If ever I've had a "Eureka!" moment in my life, that was it.

When my "home group" decided to go back to physical meetings again, I finally realised that those people who I had been sharing my life issues with over the months of my post-cancer life really did not care about me. One of the regular groups I attended on zoom decided suddenly, by a show of hands, to return to physical meetings. At least 3 of us were still clinically vulnerable and shielding; we felt minimized and dismissed as gleeful AA members chattered on about getting back to "real meetings" and how they missed the hugs and coffees together.

I wrote a letter to inter-group to express my dismay at how this "return to normality" had been handled, and also asked that the subject of vulnerable/disabled AA members during the pandemic and beyond needed to be addressed; zoom meetings had revealed the unmet needs of many people in society; women at home with children or looking after sick/disabled family members, those with reduced mobility, blindness; many people were so glad to have that support via their computers. I received no reply. My guess is that they thought it was somehow challenging to their structure but not worth discussing; the "problem" would be covered by tradition 4

"Each group should be autonomous, except in matters affecting other groups or AA as a whole".

That tradition is a great "let out" for AA; the individual doesn't stand much chance in getting heard.

I thought I had grown up before this, but the callousness with which I was treated at this time finally allowed me to hear the other shoe drop.

 I wasn't even very angry to begin with; I felt relieved in so many ways. It felt like I had touched the real core of my understanding about the false, flimsy fellowship structure that I had once thought would be a solid pillar of support for the rest of my life. I decided there would be no more bloody zoom meetings (which had become intrusive in our family home), serenity prayers, step meetings, Big Book readings, endless re-runs of negative stories with no real insight or purpose.

What came next was a huge adrenalin rush. I read everything I could about alternative routes to "recovery" and joined some online groups for people leaving AA and de-programming. Books like "The Sober Truth" by Lance Dodes MD, "Recover!" by Stanton Peele (and I watched many of his podcasts), "Her Best-kept Secret" by Gabrielle Glaser and "Alcoholics Anonymous; Cult or Cure?" by Charles Bufe. And many more. TV documentaries that dealt with cults also grabbed my attention; the identifying markers of being in a cult and being "brainwashed" resonated with me. I decided to write about the process as I saw it, from my own experience of 34 years in and out of AA and fellowship programmes. At first, I thought I was wasting my time, that there were thousands of stories like mine already out there.

Then I told myself that if I didn't write my story, that would be one less voice against the AA majority. I've always been a fighter for the underdog and this seemed to me a fight worth getting involved in. There are millions of us who have had enough of being preached at by AA, dismissed as "troublemakers" whenever we question anything and who have been sidelined for speaking out. I had to leave in order to feel safe enough to begin writing about it. The brainwashing of 34 years still needs eradicating, and it is a slow process; but it is possible, and I feel so much better.

I'm sure that other leavers have similar stories; the self-realization of the authentic voice returning after being repressed by fear of non-conformity to the group structure. There was a sense of expansion as I left the "disease model" behind and realised I had been enmeshed in a deliberate lie. This was followed, of course, by the come-down…. naturally. It had to happen. When it did, my inner critic had a field day.

"How could you have been duped for 34 years?", it shouted. I didn't sponsor anyone, didn't go to conventions, only held minor posts (chair of a meeting being the 'highest'), only went to 2 or 3 meetings a week at the end of my time (in the rooms, before Covid) …. but that's still a big connection. How come I didn't see this delusion for what it was/is? Me, of all people, a cynic by nature, a non-religious person who believed in a force for good, but who also knew that evil does exist in the world. "I'm no fool!" I cried to myself.

This lasted for quite a few weeks and I was fortunate in having a good therapist who had already seen me through my cancer and my family estrangement issues. I was able to talk things though and unravel it all; the shame, the guilt, the feelings of stupidity and ignorance; the anger (for it had surfaced very quickly after the initial euphoria of leaving AA) at being badly treated; the abuse at the treatment centre (my own and others experiences).

It was like a Christmas cracker of issues that had been hidden from me for 34 years. My exit from AA had been happening for years, through all my questioning of sponsors behaviours, letters to inter-group, trying to bring up topics that got dismissed out of hand by "old-timers", I can see now that I was trying to make a silk purse out of a sow's ear. It was never going to work for me, because basically I never fully believed in it.

At the end, I reduced my zoom meetings from 5 a week (I was doing more zoom meetings than I had done live meetings, a kind of compulsion whereby I needed to make totally sure that meetings really were not working for me) then to 3, then to 2, then just down to 1 Women's meeting. I was asked to do a main share at this (on zoom) and it turned out to be my final meeting. Something just snapped in me after I had finished talking; I got a lot of share-backs, adulation from newcomers about my 34 years sobriety (which I felt really uncomfortable about) and some dismal looks from women who I could sense were so lost in their own misery that my words just went over their heads. And it all felt so very WRONG.

I tried to go to another meeting the next day. I set up my laptop in plenty of time for an early morning meeting I had been attending for several months. I just couldn't bring myself to log in. I had experienced something similar in the past, a sort of "shut down", when I had a nervous breakdown brought on by a toxic work environment and a bullying boss. In that instance, I got ready for work as usual, picked up my car keys....and then sat back on the sofa and froze. I couldn't move.

I never went back to work for 6 months, and then I eventually left once I realised that however much I wanted that environment to change, it wouldn't. A big dose of reality had flooded me, and I put my mental health first – both in that work experience and in my final understanding of where I stood in my relation to AA. This was the end.

The weight of the "imaginary illness" and the "fellowship of other alcoholics" was lifted immediately and has faded away. It feels good, it feels real, it feels timely. I continue to have one-to-one therapy and I know I can still be "triggered" when I see the rosy version of AA depicted in the media or on TV shows. Celebrities seem to be coming forward by the ton to pledge their allegiance to "the programme". I can't run away from that, but I can protest it and write about it.

I no longer take my "inventory" every day, I don't read daily spiritual readings, and I give myself total permission to waste time whenever I need to. AA meetings and "service" fill up a lot of empty space, which is often a consequence of giving up drink and drugs. I don't "hand it over" anymore; I don't torture myself with recriminations about all the "alcoholics out there" who I am not helping. If you want to waste time and energy, then join a 12-step fellowship programme – it's a masterclass in diversion of your life skills and teaches you to conform with such alacrity that you remain forever in gratitude and servitude, unaware that life is passing you by.

My family and friends come first, my social conscience is in a healthy place and I fully understand that I will see-saw between moods of light and dark; I'm human and I'm not different from everyone else (AA says we are) because I had a drink problem. I had trauma issues; I continue to work with them and I fully accept that some of that will never be totally "resolved". I've learned to live with that. Going without a drink for a long time in AA does not necessarily make you a better person; in many cases it just produces a repressed desire to have a drink, because no real issues can ever be really addressed in an AA meeting. It puts on a good show, but now I can see backstage where all the sandbags and faded costumes are. To take the theatrical analogy further, there is always a prompt in the wings, ready to whisper your next line.

I am still angry at AA and the programming they carry out with impunity. It has definitely had a long-term negative impact on my life. Such a powerful organisation needs to be publicly accountable and regulated by independent authorities. If there is any disease-concept that needs to be discussed, then it ought to be the disease of AA; or how a religious cult, based on a decades old badly written book became an acceptable form of help for millions of people with severe trauma experiences and mental health issues.

 To challenge it is to incur the wrath of millions of people who swear it has saved their lives. To suggest it is flawed, harmful at the very least and often dangerous is considered a sort of heresy, often by people who have no idea what goes in AA meeting rooms and how it fails so many desperate people Is there a pill for that Doctor?

Chapter 6
The AA way of life

I only attended one "conference"; a one-day event in Bristol (which is where I was born, grew up and did a lot of drinking). It has a large fellowship population and many connections with treatment centres, plus, hundreds of fellowship meetings.

Conventions are propaganda events for the 12 step programmes; exercises in crowd recruitment and morale boosting, a way to get "the message" over to a large audience with speakers, group meetings and the chance to purchase vast amounts of AA funded literature (if you put money in the pot, then you are paying for the literature; Grapevine inc. is the publishing arm of World Service Inc.)

I describe it as a joyless kind of Holiday Camp, and the only games being played are usually sexual ones, as predators seem to love these get-togethers, using them as speed-dating centres. I went to only one, but I have known other "alcoholics" who have been to many conferences and would agree with this opinion.

As an introvert, I am very sensitive to large, voluble groups of people, constant stimulation and conversational interaction. In other words, I experience "overload" fairly quickly at events (unless I'm performing on stage; that is a very different experience). Also, a stream of AA shares is perhaps the most tedious and unhelpful way to inspire a feeling of wellness in me. The conference I attended was held in a large student union building and featured speakers from all over the world. I left after an hour, feeling bored and disconnected after listening to a dead-pan would-be comedian from the USA regaling us with florid tales of his epic drinking bouts. Yuk. Rather than a feeling of "experience, strength and hope", I left, nursing a headache from too much cigarette smoke and continuous forced laughter.

I took myself off for a decent coffee and spent a lovely afternoon in record shops, book shops, the museum and art gallery and ended up in a charity shop where I bought some amazing clothes for under £15. That was in my early recovery days, when I had just left the treatment centre. I wasn't missed at the conference, and frankly I didn't care. This ambivalence toward AA and fellowship life had been with me from the start and I was often "pulled up" about it by other AA members who often said I was not committed and that I "isolated".

I want to talk about that; in the treatment centre, I was given that label by one of the counsellors. She accused me of "isolating" every time I wanted to be on my own for a bit of space after being with a barrel load of broken monkeys all day (I include myself in the barrel, but enough is enough sometimes). I disagreed with her, and still do.

Individuals who misuse drink/drugs are as likely to need "space" as anyone else and I resented being expected to do something that did not help my mental health – that is, spending too much time with people resulting in a feeling of fragmentation and anxiety. A trained health professional would have picked up that my need for solitude was part of my character and not a "defect" as the programme would have had me believe.

"Defects" of character (in AA terminology) are just human characteristics that we all share.

I was fast realising that being in AA and going to daily meetings was neither "fixing" me or helping me to progress. If anything, it continued to slow me down and distract me from thinking about what I wanted to do next in my life, it stopped me from planning and drained my energies.

Living the AA life seemed to me, even then, to consist of a constant round of meetings, sponsorship, step work, making amends, feeling ashamed and going for coffee with other AA members where the conversation revolved around the "wonderful promises of recovery" and what a special race of people we were, looking down on the "normals" as most members called them. Exclusivity is another trait of a "cult" structure that seeks to be divisive.

Race is worth looking at too, as another issue. AA, at that time in Bristol, comprised mainly white people. I used to wonder where people who weren't white went to meetings; I only met a few people of colour in AA; there may be studies on this somewhere but I have not found any yet related to that historical period in Bristol.

The ridiculousness of identifying ourselves as somehow "different" from other human beings who struggle with similar life issues, is a marker of a cult organisation. I did meet more damaged people than I'd ever met before, that much is true. In my first 2 years in AA (including treatment) I experienced more drama, arguments, unpleasant interactions and angry/tearful exchanges than I had in the previous 10 years prior to joining. Granted, some of that was due to my own raw, emotional state and my vulnerability living without the crutch of drinking – but not all of it, much of it was toxic interchange that I could have done without.

I found that the more I hung out with groups of AA people, the worse I felt about myself. I got to breaking point one August Bank holiday weekend, when I was feeling very low, and I accepted an invitation from a theatrical friend to go on a weekend healing retreat in Anglesey (which was actually a bit "cultish" too but the place was beautiful; a large house in fabulous landscaped gardens and I would get free meals and accommodation , it seemed like a good idea for a much needed break, and I was strapped for cash– but I could hear my Dad's constant mantra "there's no such thing as a free lunch!".

The alternative was a miserable weekend in the city with the prospect of the Big Book Saturday night meeting and various other day/evening meetings, coffee with the AA crew and maybe a movie….

My 13th stepping boyfriend had cast me off and left me with unpaid bills from the flat we had shared. I felt sad, lonely, and needed a change. Off we went to Anglesey in my friends battered old Vauxhall and we had a great time!

I did yoga, meditated, sang songs and chanted, went canoeing, ate wonderful vegetarian food, had a one-on-one talk with the "guru in chief" who was very calm and funny and did not try to lure me into the compound and give him all my money. He obviously could see that I had none! In fact, I got a lot from talking with him about life, energy, purpose and all kinds of things. I felt glad that I had taken the risk to do something different. And part of me felt that I had "betrayed" AA.

When I returned, my AA friends made no bones about telling me how foolish I was, that I was playing a "dangerous game" with my sobriety. Fear is the overarching emotion that supports the AA structure. Somehow, I was able to hang on to the sense of vitality that I had rediscovered in myself while I was at the healing retreat; I would not let the AA negativity squash that.

I made plans on paper, outlined some goals and did not talk about them to anyone in AA. I applied to college in Bath as a mature student to take a Performing Arts diploma. I got accepted and I received a grant; it felt fantastic to be in control of my life again and I was looking forward to a new phase of life, rather than backwards to my drinking days. I was pulling away from the cloying, claustrophobic world of fellowships which seemed only interested in keeping me standing still; it felt liberating.

It wasn't easy. I still doubted myself a lot; I continued going to meetings, but by then I had found some "Women in AA" and Lesbian & Gay AA" groups at which I felt more comfortable and safer. Even so, I began to limit the time I spent going to meetings and I reduced my coffee/chat meet-ups with AA members which were eating away at my finances and my creative brain. The repetition, the repetition, the repetition!!!!

There are so many people in AA who just want to talk you to death. I think it has the largest community of narcissistic egotists (aside from governments and religions of course) Yes, I was in AA! it can be another form of addiction! A platform for talking, talking, talking about self, but not in a healing way. However, I also think there are many lovely and deluded people caught in the trap of the programme.

I'm a good listener as well as a good talker and I was often "trapped" by old-timers who wanted to fill my head with their own particular brand of the message of AA. So, I frequently found myself overwhelmed and frozen into silence when maybe I should have spoken out. It's hard when you don't have sufficient confidence as an individual in a group of people who all seem to know what they are doing (it's a fake; they don't know any better than anyone else).

By the time Friday night came around, I usually found myself utterly exhausted by a week of AA. These indicators, I see now, are huge "red flags" for me. Nowadays, I would not consider spending so large an amount of time on "other people's stuff". It's unhealthy and unproductive for both parties.

The re-telling of stories, constant self-examination, the gossip, the comparisons with others sobriety – the AA community is not so much a fellowship of like-minded people as a vast network of lost, needy, brainwashed folk, desperately trying to get fixed by someone else who at best is struggling equally and at worst, could actually do them some harm. I never would have thought I could feel so strongly against AA; it is as if the scales have fallen from my eyes; when I was "in the rooms" I knew something was not sitting right with me, but it was only when I left completely that clarity returned. The cumulative effect of 34 years of group-think has a legacy that I am still confronting.

I do not believe that people with alcohol/drug problems need to live the "AA way of life" in order to get and stay well. It is ONE option, and it is a very poor one in my view. Moving forward and living life to the full is what we all want, whether or not we drink/use drugs or stay sober or teetotal; whatever you want to call it. My view is that AA keeps you "stuck". Like a dysfunctional family that doesn't want you to change, AA keeps its claws in you, telling you repeatedly that you cannot do it alone or that if you leave, you will certainly die.

This is not only untrue, it is highly dangerous; this dogmatic stance causes vulnerable people to relapse which can lead to death, which seems as if AA was right all along…. except they weren't; people often relapse from AA because they feel they haven't lived up to the standards expected of them, or they haven't followed the "tough love" advice of their tyrannical sponsor (who is only another person who has had drink/drug misuse issues, not a trained professional). I have witnessed extremely vulnerable people walking out of meetings after being publicly shamed for not doing enough "service", and then drinking on it. Despicable behaviour, and hardly the loving picture AA likes to present to the media and "outsiders".

As I continued to take more risks in my life, met new acquaintances and friends outside "the rooms" my innate confidence returned. I had agency in my life again, I was able to make things happen without continual reference to the 12-step programme or unwanted advice from AA members.

I was living my life without drink or drugs (neither of which I craved once I had given up), I was making mistakes, having emotional meltdowns, picking myself back up, getting help from friends and other sources when I needed it. Yet I still kept going to meetings. I am still surprised that I stayed in for so long. I nurtured the hope, for a very long time, that if I only waited long enough, something would happen. Hanging on too long, in any situation had always been something I did and I needed to address it in order to fully regain my self-hood.

Remaining in AA was no different than staying too long in a crap job, or hoping that a relationship would improve when I knew it was in vain. The futility was part of my "pattern", which told me that it wasn't up to me, I had to wait for someone/something outside of me to give me permission.

I left AA the first time when I moved back to Bristol, met someone, began a fruitful performing life, had a daughter and a new home. Temporarily, my AA life was over. I didn't go to any fellowships for 13 years. I became involved in the Spiritualist Church (another organisation I eventually came away from due to the preponderance of charlatans and emotional vampires).

I am definitely attracted to groups of "seekers", but they are often filled with lonely, damaged people and misguided rebels such as myself. I'm not ashamed to say I've trusted far too many people too quickly and had some very steep learning curves. I do not despise people for "seeking", but I do believe in learning more about my own psyche, about why I cannot trust myself enough to stick to my own goals and decisions without feeling guilty. That's a big learning curve. There are far too many people who manipulate that, particularly in organisations like AA.

Singing, music, dance and theatre were my healers, as well as my wonderful family of my husband and daughter and my step-son, and that continues to be the case to this day (though my dancing days have been curtailed due to herpetic paralysis).

I'm not keen on "joining" things anymore; the famous crack by Groucho Marx applies to me "I don't want to join any club that would have me as a member". I like my own company, yet I am also gregarious and for me, it is all about balance. When I stopped drinking, I still had a need for social acceptance, and support too, which I thought AA would give me. I don't feel like that anymore. I'm not the same person that walked into a dark church hall one Thursday night in the late 80's and pulled up an uncomfortable chair and got smoked out by 30 "alcoholics".

The AA way of life is certainly not for me. It never was, but when there are no other avenues presented or made available, then it is very likely you will give it a go, as I did.

Society needs a wide-ranging resource base for alcohol and addiction issues. Ones that do not involve profit or exploitation by a few powerful companies or programmes. The diversity of help must match the diversity of the people using the services. AA, as a religious, dogmatic structure is not the model we should be aspiring to in the 21st Century.

Its power needs to be challenged, its practices regulated, its literature up-dated; it needs to be publicly accountable particularly in the area of predatory behaviour of group members and it needs to encourage open discussion of other methods of treatment and help besides the 12-step model, so as not to leave struggling group members with no options other than prayer. As it is so fond of telling its members, AA needs to be "right-sized".

Chapter 7
Keep coming back

In AA, a "relapse" (return to using alcohol/drugs) is a sip of a drink, a pain-killer, a liqueur chocolate, a goulash made with red wine, an inadvertently consumed glass of wine at a wedding or a funeral; the list is bloody endless. Once you have "yielded to temptation", your hard-won sobriety is not only compromised, often the slate of sober days is completely wiped clean and you are back at base, ashamed, penitent and back to Step 1, shamefully claiming your "1 Day Sober chip".

Relapsing is a serious issue if, like me, you were a very heavy drinker, and if, like me, you really didn't want to return to that life, then AA putting the fear of something into me seemed helpful – at the beginning. But ultimately it is a chain of pain that only serves to impose guilt and control on someone who is already struggling to live life without drink/drugs. It can, and does, cause people to go on benders and die; a suicide in reality. AA calls drinking a "slow suicide", but there are too many of the faster variety connected with AA for my liking.

AA will then turn around and say "you see, they left AA and look what happened!" in a sanctimonious avoidance of any responsibility. Or, even worse; "they just didn't get the programme". I've sat in many meetings where the death of a well-known, longtime member of the group or region has died, and there was a definite cognitive dissonance going on.

People would at first share their sadness, but it would be tinged with a coldness and a punitive tone. Many of the group members would attend the funerals and give "support" to the grieving family members. I knew of one such family who expressly requested that no AA members attend the funeral; this was discussed of course at the meeting and the resulting group think opinion was "they wouldn't be able to cope with the fact that he/she had not worked the programme".

The arrogance of AA in the face of death and suicide particularly is astonishing. The dead person would then only be mentioned at future meetings as a severe warning to newcomers, if at all; their sad demise attributed to their own failure at working the steps. The compassion button was switched off.

Each person that finds AA is damaged in some way; very often at the end of their physical and emotional resilience after years of alcohol/drug misuse, abuse and poor life choices. Trauma experienced in families, society and relationships have made them extremely vulnerable. Their template for living has been warped, sometimes broken. Focused, caring guidance is required to help put the pieces back together.

"If you are willing to go to any lengths…." Says AA. Most of us are willing when we get to AA. Most of us didn't know there was anything else particularly back in the 80's when I started going, and there is nothing more enticing to a tired, hungry fish than a worm on a hook. If the programme endorsed a finite course that would help drinkers to move on, go forward and feel empowered it would go some way to redressing the balance of their present monopoly of the treatment business (for it is a very lucrative business).

However, staying stuck on an endless programme for life, a conveyor-belt philosophy that entails enslavement to rituals, prayers and continual service does not resemble a wholesome design for living. One can never be "cured" with this system. AA believes there is no cure, that an alcoholic is always going to be an alcoholic.

Going back to the relapse list at the start of this chapter, I believe that there is not one person in the world who can truly stand up in an AA meeting and claim a day's sobriety. Therefore, all the power-games and war-stories of "old-timers" and bullying sponsors are really just pissing in the wind. Why take notice of any of them? My own stories and troubles very likely bored the pants off many people who had to sit through them, which is so very like a drunk in a bar regaling anyone who will listen with humorous elaborate anecdotes that have no beginning and no end. Of course, there is a similarity. AA is a dry bar stocked with tales of misery; straight, no chaser.

Interestingly, "serial relapsers" (and there are millions) in AA speak of the "revolving door of recovery".

Many relapse with the express purpose of "coming back" through that door to experience the "love bombing" ("so glad you've had the courage to come back" ….); or conversely, the masochistic thrill of being told "you've proved to yourself that you can't do it without us, so now shut your mouth and open your ears") AA members have a craving to be needed, it is part of the manipulation of an unaware mind and the egotistical desire to believe that our association with a powerful group will make us "safe" and also absolve us of the need to look within in a healthy way.

AA members want to be needed FOREVER and if it requires that they either love bomb or shame a relapser into submission, then that is a cost to their character that they are willing to pay. They are ok with that; and any doubts as to their behaviour will be swiftly handed over to their higher power, whether that is a "god of their understanding" or satan. I often wonder if there is a satanic sect of AA, as there are many "atheist/agnostic" groups. They all peddle the same jargon and they all require strict allegiance to conformity with the groupthink.

Most people who join AA only make a year of sobriety within the fellowship. Millions just leave and either go back to drinking, change their lifestyles, seek professional qualified help or grow out of it. Yes, millions of people just grow out of it when they find purpose and healing in their lives, without any sort of "programme". And many, like me, leave after decades of "in and out" membership of AA and find they need to de-programme themselves after years of brainwashing and wasted hours.

Relapse is so very common because AA is like a "fix", it works for a while but ultimately it doesn't last. That is why "keep coming back, it works if you work it" (trotted out like a child's rhyme at the conclusion of every meeting) is barked out so enthusiastically. It is the perennial child whistling in the dark to keep the bogeyman away.

You must (but there are no musts in AA, only suggestions! Says the BIG BOOK!) return to a never-ending cycle of meetings, sponsorship, conferences, conventions and interminable ramblings of people who cannot even remember their last drink/drug because it was so long ago.

Tradition 5 of AA suggests "each group has but one primary purpose – to carry its message to the alcoholic who still suffers" – and this is the "recruitment drive" step of AA. It's not about the individual getting well and moving forward, it is about getting more members into the AA 12-step programme. Keep it simple; the pyramid scheme is a tried and tested one.

When I gave up drinking, I was done with it. I drank excessively for a long time, got into a fair bit of trouble over the years, experienced a lot of pain because of it and I don't wish it on anyone. I have no idea if I reached a "rock bottom" (AA will tell you that you will always go further down if you leave the fellowship). In many ways, I think I've had lots of "rock bottom" times in my life, just like any other human being.

I knew I didn't want to drink any more and I stopped. Unluckily for me, I found AA. I believe I could have saved myself much anguish and drama if I had only gone to my therapy sessions. But I did join and that is the way of it. I was not overly concerned about relapsing, as many people are. I didn't suffer cravings when I stopped and I felt no desire to take a drink. I also denied myself fun and interaction with "normal" people in the early days of my enmeshment with AA, so the relapsing message must have found a resting place in my psyche. I became overly risk-averse, unable to branch out sometimes when I could have. I regret that loss and I grieve it.

I've always felt very compassionate toward people who have relapsed and who then proceeded to berate themselves in the meeting arena. I cringed for them as some harsh critic with "sober time" would remind them that they had not "handed it over yet" and were still "egocentric and unable to grasp this simple programme". This condescending attitude, prevalent in AA is evidence of the "moral weakness" aspect of drinking that supports the disease model.

If alcoholics believe themselves to have a disease, then they are not responsible for any misdeeds they commit in their lives. It's a bit of a catch 22 situation; "If I'm bad, it's not my fault because I have a disease. But if I'm morally weak, then I need to get help and see how I can make changes and be responsible for my drinking and my life". AA supports both points of view, but only by "suggestion".

This standpoint naturally leads to interpretation and confusion. The ambivalence and lack of accountability on AA's part, leads to the oft-quoted phrase "AA is a broad church; we accept allcomers". Again, this can sound very reassuring to a newcomer. The day-to-day lived experience of the group meetings is very different. And please note, that this phrase, ubiquitous in meetings I have attended, calls AA "a church". It is a religion despite its protestations to the contrary.

Experimentation with drink and drugs is as old as mankind. So is "maturing out" of excessive usage. We grow up; hopefully and all of us at different rates. I have come to regard AA as a kindergarten that compels people to repeatedly sing "the wheels on the bus" when they actually need to be booming out a few verses of punk, blues, rock and jazz. Or whatever music turns you on!

Relapse stories are common and anecdotal in meetings; and everyone knows a serial relapser who just can't seem to get "the message". That's because it doesn't work for that person and is a failure of the programme, not the person. They are not getting what they need and no one is allowed to point them in a different direction (however at the end of my AA time, I sent private zoom messages during the meetings to any newcomers who seemed to be hesitant about the "message" they were hearing")

In my first year in AA, a man used to come and go in meetings with a half-bottle of whisky in his coat pocket some weeks and then arrive smart and suited for a month or so. He was permanently caught "in the swing door". He often sat by me and I always talked to him whether he was drunk or sober. Old-timers discouraged me from talking to him when he was drunk. My nature drew me to talk with him and to try and find out what was going on in his life, why he felt he had to keep drinking to try and solve his problems. I thought this was the foundation of the AA message.

Eventually, he stopped coming and I bumped into him, in the street a few months later. He seemed very well; he said he had joined his local church, changed his job and felt like AA had not helped him at all. When I told AA friends that I had talked with him and that he was doing fine, they all sneered; "he's in denial! He'll be back!" they chanted.

I saw him again 13 years later at a music festival in Bristol – he was still doing marvelously well and was pleased to see me. He told me that I had been one of the few people in AA that had shown him kindness and hadn't judged him for coming to meetings drunk. I had to tell him that I was still in the fellowship (I felt ashamed at that) but meeting up with him was another light-bulb moment for me that eventually led to my mind lighting up like Crystal Palace, so I'm glad we crossed paths again.

There were several suicides I knew about in my early AA days (and in later years, but these initial ones seem to linger as I was raw and very impressionable). One was an elderly gentleman (mid-70's) who I had come to know through a regular meeting which I chaired for a time. I remember hearing him talk at one weekend meeting; he had been in and out of AA for years and had recently de-toxed in hospital and was taking some heavy-duty medication. He sounded sad, lonely, despairing, and his voice was paper-thin, little more than a whisper. I felt he was hardly "there".

I felt a well-spring of compassion for this man. When he had finished speaking, there was a very brief pause before someone jumped in to share about how angry they were about a parking ticket they had received that day. It was so dismissive and insensitive. After the meeting, I smiled at the sad man and went over to him but he didn't want to talk. He shuffled out, whilst loud laughter and chatter filled the room, as was usual at the end of a meeting.

A few days later, I found out that the man had died; he had taken an overdose at some point after that meeting. Because I was still "fresh in" and open to so many new people and shares, that incident upset me deeply and I've never forgotten it. Something was lacking in that room for that man

– empathy, compassion, a friendly hand to offer some practical help; I had felt its' lack.

I know AA people will say "well you can't blame AA for that! He would probably have done it anyway" However, I disagree. There have been too many cases of relapses and suicides related to being in AA to ignore the connection. Patterns of behaviour show us things about people in groups; they can reveal what can be expected so that plans can be put in place to reduce harmful actions and behaviours.

An AA group is only as strong as its members and their "group conscience". It's a very moveable feast due to the constant flow of people at different stages of neediness and "recovery". No regulations exist to offer alternative help to people such as the man I mention above. ("Each group is autonomous", tradition 4 of AA)

AA has an abundance of publications; read as many as you like (and there are hundreds, produced by Grapevine Inc. the publishing wing of AA) and you won't find any other help besides the 12 steps, prayer and 12 step model for treatment. For this alone, AA needs to be monitored and regulated by an independent medical body.

"The sine qua non of the healthy group experience is that it not become an ultimate preoccupation in itself, but that it lead you to re-immerse yourself in

life outside the group with renewed vigour, health and success" (Stanton Peele, "The Truth about Addiction & Recovery).

Finding renewed purpose in life was one of the biggest challenges when I stopped drinking. For me, seeking meaningful and rewarding activities became my goal, not living in a structure of sickness that tells people they are powerless and that they can never be cured. "Keep coming back" is a powerful negative reinforcement message that you are giving to yourself, whilst at the same time attempting to re-empower yourself in life choices.

What enduring freedom or liberation can you experience if you cannot proclaim yourself cured and become a self-actualized person? Whether that means abstinence or moderation or medication-model therapy, it is ultimately up to the individual, not an outdated religious programme that uses your vulnerabilities against your best interests, which I believe AA does.

Over 34 years in/out of AA, I have inadvertently ingested alcohol in mince-pies, nut roasts, trifle, chocolates, sauerkraut, vinegar, cough medicines, sauces and by picking up the wrong drink at a gathering or at a gig/festival. By the AA dictum, this makes me a "serial relapser". Hilarious. I often used to hang onto my drink for grim death at a party or an event in case I got spiked or I took someone else's drink by mistake. That's just crazy making! Mistakes were made; and I didn't go on a binge or end up in "jails, institutions or death".

In the 30's, when Bill W wrote his Big Book, there was a serious lack of help for heavy drinkers; (hospital de-tox or the Church); I think all lapsed members of AA would agree with that. Bill W and Dr. Bob Smith provided a religious solution for its time; and they also capitalized on it. It was that simple. Prohibition and temperance were part of their social fabric. Abstinence and over-indulgence go hand in hand in a depressed society.

To still be relying on the 12-step programme and fellowship model as the most recognizable and available treatment in the 21st Century is no indication of progress in our treatment of alcohol/drug misuse. As I write this, I can hear internalized AA voices in the gallery of my mind shouting, "it's lasted so long because it works!"

Actually, no, it doesn't work for everyone and it only works long-term for about 5-8% of people who try it. It certainly has big drawbacks for women who are liable (more than men) to be sexually harassed, 13th stepped and even raped and murdered (see Monica Richardson's film, The 13th Step) There are now many evidence based scientific approaches managing alcohol misuse and the research continues apace.

I am at a point in my life where I am happy to hold up my hand and say "I'm recovered" – if that means anything at all! I would never have dared to say that whilst I was in AA. The word "recovery" now has little meaning to me, other than a way to get a car to a garage when it has broken down. The problem I had with leaving AA was not the actual leaving. That was quite easy, I was ready to go and had been detaching within the fellowship for many years.

What I am working with now, is the residue of the programme; the brainwashing, the slogans, the negative responses to normal life situations, the occasional guilt of not attending meetings (that just pops up like a bad penny now and again, particularly when I'm up against a tough situation). Plus, the anger and grief over the wasted time.

I approach de-programming like anything else, with all the self-reliance I have learned from life and with help from friends and my therapist. I'm also a member of several social media de-programming groups (though I am still very wary of any groups – "take what you like and leave the rest" says AA – I wish I'd never taken any of it!) and I access a lot of very helpful podcasts and YouTube clips.

There are some amazingly courageous people out there who have left AA and other cults and who are telling their true stories at last. I've read a lot of scientific, medical and philosophical literature. I've explored mysticism, spiritualism and many other areas of "healing" (which I was always advised by AA to refrain from).

Cancer has taught me a lot, as well as the illnesses and deaths of close family and friends; it just comes with the territory of getting older. Getting old is a privilege that many don't get.

I no longer have to stand up in a seedy room and say "my name is Marilyn and I'm an alcoholic". No thank you. AA has had the monopoly on "recovery" for far too long. Many millions applaud its "success stories". And many millions do not and are harmed by this model of "recovery". There are a growing number of AA leavers now speaking out; it is indicative of a critical change and new thinking regarding an age-old problem in a modern society, one which, like Covid, is not going away anytime soon.

Chapter 8

The AA Couple

A frequent phenomenon I came across in AA was the zealous "AA couple". Usually, these are married couples (not always); often a product of early sobriety matching (leaving lifetime partners to hitch up with a new AA man or woman who mirrors their recovery trajectory) who then go on to become Big Book/fellowship fanatics, intent on "carrying the message" and recruiting as many new members as possible. They give up their jobs, their family connections, their "old lives"; they live the slogan; "put AA before everything else" so fully that it is as if they are starting their lives from scratch.

They commonly dominate at one particular meeting, and sometimes whole regional areas. They have a tyrannical, regulatory hold on groups and preside over how they function. The men tend to be "club leaders" and the women act as a "mother hen" (of course this can work in all genders, it's just my experience is that of the hetero "norm" that was evident in the years I spent in AA).

Under the guise of "sponsorship",(mentoring/supporting a new member to work through the steps of the 12-step programme) these couples can rule with impunity, force out members they don't like (or ensure that they do not hold any positions of influence in the group), engage in malicious, covert bullying by being hardline "step merchants" and they can put a full stop to any open discussions or challenges to the group structure, particularly at group conscience meetings. They regularly interfere with peoples lives outside of the group, citing their involvement as "helping you stay on the programme".

They typically take on higher posts (Group Service Representative, Area Service Representative) and attend many 12 step conferences, often invited to speak all over the world. They are invariably financially well-off and seem to have vast amounts of time on their hands to spend in the service of AA. In effect, they are the "marketing marriages" wing of the fellowship way of life.

During Zoom/Covid, I saw clearly how damaging this "double-whammy "of sobriety worked. A couple with almost 70 years sobriety between them had a strong presence in several of the groups I attended. They appeared on screen, side by side, immediately creating a powerful position from which to "work". This couple had met in a hospital detox situation and both came from very rigid religious backgrounds (good conformist material for AA).

They went to fellowship meetings in the hospital and when they were discharged continued their "mission" in the AA community "outside". They were "missionaries" in the sense that they were evangelical in their objective to spread the word of AA. Couples like this gain many "sponsees" and can completely control an AA community. I've seen it happen.

This particular couple had a fairly stereotypical marriage; Sarah had been a "homemaker". Graham had been the "breadwinner". They each had families with ex-partners. He had been a serial philanderer whose family now had nothing to do with him (even though he'd been sober for 30 years plus, there was no advancement in his relations with family members – he was 100% an AA man, giving up all his time to the programme and carrying the message to "the still-suffering alcoholic").

Sarah had a solid base of young female AA acolytes who hung on her every word and went to endless meetings, producing Step 4s on demand for their "clan mother". Her own daughter had serious alcohol misuse issues and Sarah constantly berated her behaviour at meetings in a cruel and judgmental way that I found very destructive. (Her daughter refused to join the fellowship, saying it was "shit") It was all very sick, but by no means unusual, and during the Zoom meetings, I took the chance to make notes of some of what they both said.

Regarding newcomers, Graham had strong feelings; "I like to see their naked fear; in fact, I love to see the whites of their eyes as they realise, they've lost everything and everyone they had through the drink – they are at rock bottom – it's then that I can do gods work"

I had been at physical AA meetings where Graham had said similar things, but it seemed more intense on Zoom and it caused a wave of revulsion in me. There were first-time attendees at that meeting and I witnessed their anxious faces, frozen on-screen, wondering what the hell they were getting into! Sarah sat serenely by his side, her penetrating, head-mistress stare seeking out any possible vulnerable prey as she nodded vigorously in agreement with her husband.

As soon as he had finished, (he "preached" for 10 minutes at least) Sarah jumped straight in to endorse his message and to promote an AA "mini-convention" (a one-day event in a church hall with 4 speakers). This was during Lockdown when strict regulations were still in place and the covid virus was killing thousands of people.

 (But hey! This is AA! We are all friends! We'll beat that nasty virus by hugging and breathing the same air for 5 hours in a stuffy Church Hall!) The convention was duly cancelled from lack of support; even stalwart AA members weren't willing to go full-lemming into Nirvana, in an attempt to carry the message.

The convention was named "Recovery is our Business", which in itself is very revealing; a pyramid scheme that needs constant "fresh meat" in order to continue to grow, expand and take over the entire treatment service sector for people seeking help with alcohol/drug misuse. Sarah smiled as she plugged the event, extolling the virtues of the speakers she had lined up to share their "experience, strength and hope" (sub-text; degradation, humiliation and ultimate supplication to God, followed by salvation as long as they continue to attend AA meetings).

This would be interspersed with lunch, sharing contact numbers, recruitment of any confused newcomers, then off everyone could go, happy and content, leaving a trail of uncovered trauma and pain with only the prospect of another AA meeting to put the holy lid back on the can of worms unleashed (which actually needs a qualified professional to do some damage limitation, then find out how the individual can best be helped).

These events are a major part of the rotten fabric of AA. A manipulators dream; often with a good smattering of predatory men, on the look-out for vulnerable women who often attend these events because they are free and who have no access to private therapy and may be on a 3-4 year waiting list for NHS counselling.

Toxic "AA couples" adore these events as they can display their wonderful sober lives together and trot out that beloved AA chestnut; "if you want what we have, you will go to any lengths to get it…." The larger conventions have considerably greater opportunities for the wealthy AA elite to ply their recovery trade of saving souls from the demon drink. This may sound like an exaggeration, a malicious swipe at people who only wish to "do good". I challenge that.

These couples do great harm and are not held to account for their power trips. The hierarchical nature of the fellowship protects them and allows them a freedom of speech and action denied to the "lower levels".

While I was writing this book, I watched the USA version of "House of Cards" (the original UK version was by Andrew Davies). I was struck by the similarity between Frank Underwood (the president, played by Kevin Spacey) and his wife Clare (played by Robin Wright) with the behaviour of AA couples. The way Frank and Clare manipulate people and situations to bolster their power base is resonant of AA couples working persistently and rigorously, sometimes under the radar, to achieve their aims. Frank and Clare's total belief in their shared direction has no basis in wanting rewarding, lasting change for the American people. Their desires stem from a narcissistic, egotistical fantasy of omnipotence that should have stopped at age 7.

The toxic AA couples I have met, without exception, are comparable – though they don't get to control the White House……but there are AA meetings on Capitol Hill and in the Houses of Parliament! The "network" of AA power spreads out, like a mycelium messaging service that eventually becomes unbreachable. Trying to question such a powerful alliance is often too dangerous to contemplate and compliance becomes so much easier, and rewarding, both financially and psychologically.

A fear-based network operates in AA via the power-hungry "co-dependent couples" and they work at creating their very own "House of Cards" under the umbrella of "spirituality". An individual attempting to question the behaviour or conduct of such couples will quickly be put into the deep-freeze of AA "conviviality" (in other words, if you dare speak up, prepare to be sent to Coventry).

When I reflect on the implications of this sort of unhealthy power within a supposedly "caring" organisation, it brings up a lot of anger, sadness and grief at how individual voices get lost in the "group think" that rules AA.

Cults often (but not always) have a charismatic, controlling leader. The toxic couples in charge bring a "happy families" element into the equation. Considering that most people who drink heavily have painful trauma-bonds with family members, it is hardly surprising that the familiarity engendered by the toxic couples feels just like home. Another House of Cards.

Chapter 9

Promises, promises

The promises of AA recovery are usually, but not always, read out at the end of a meeting (sometimes at the start). Presented in a points format for greater impact, many members know this litany off by heart. It is the "high note" of the programme and is the gold standard for those wishing to live the AA way of life.

In this chapter, I'm going to break the promises down one by one, outlining the sub-text of each point, as I understand it. I've parroted this list hundreds of times and it is another of the brainwashing texts of AA that I am releasing myself from.

"We are going to know a new freedom and a new happiness"

Firstly, "we", not you. As soon as you join AA you are part of the group-think mentality. This phrase is the cream on the cake, it is very appealing if your life has been a mess for a while. It is the start of the "commercial" – all new, all packaged and ready to go. It is a statement, a tall-order, it implies that it will most definitely happen; if you work the "programme".

"We will not regret the past nor wish to shut the door on it"

I interpret this as "don't reflect too much about what's gone before, but please share endlessly about it at meetings"; it is contradictory. Also, the "door" only has "AA" written on it; not harm-reduction methods, therapy, CBT, hypnosis, yoga, mysticism, other religions etc. Individual enquiry and different practices to help with alcohol/drug misuse are not encouraged or discussed.

"We will comprehend the word serenity and we will know peace"

This assumes you have never known serenity or peace, and also sounds like a command. My life, like everyone else's, is complex, by turns calm or disrupted by outside events; I struggle with difficult situations and feelings. AA cannot guarantee serenity or peace. That is down to me.

"No matter how far down the scale we have gone, we will see how our experience can benefit others"

There it is again; the royal "we". The implication is that you are broken, in need of repair and will owe it to others to help them change once you are "mended". Why? We are individuals. If, as AA claims "attraction rather than promotion" is the key to AA success then surely "we" do not have to feel responsible for every person who joins the organisation? Or do we? Where is the balance between getting well and expecting AA as a regulated body, to be accountable for its members well-being? The hook is now deeply in; "we" help you get well, "you" then go and recruit others. It is very much like a pyramid scheme.

"That feeling of uselessness and self-pity will disappear"

This a huge claim, and in my experience is utter bullshit. Each of us needs to pity ourselves, and a period of boredom/discontent as a human being is natural, particularly during times of extreme change. These feelings are often the pre-cursors to taking positive action or thinking creatively of something in a new way. When a child says "I'm bored", it is always a mistake to immediately give it something to "do".

It is far better to acknowledge the child's feelings of boredom and see if they can pull out of the tail-spin on their own (for a while at least) This particular phrase implies AA is the panacea for your existential angst – it is not. It definitely fills up time though, I'll give it that.

"We will lose interest in selfish things and gain interest in our fellows"

Another assumption; that you never cared for anyone other than yourself when you were drinking/using. I have rarely met anyone (in AA or outside of it) who has not cared for anyone at all. There are levels of good and bad behaviour, and some people definitely are more selfish than others. However, what I am interested in highlighting here is the amount of guilt that this phrase engenders in an individual. Guilt is perhaps the emotion most frequently manipulated in the fellowship world; along with fear, it can keep you in thrall to unhealthy conditions for decades.

 For example, AA members (myself included) are often discouraged from putting their own lives and wellbeing before a meeting. Family events, relationships, concerts, pleasurable pursuits holidays, hobbies – all must take second place to AA. This gives a sense of dissociation, a feeling of not being "present" in your own life.

This "promises" phrase is an insidious betrayal of your own lived experience and "asks" you to sacrifice your personhood and time to "the group", on a regular, ongoing basis.

"Self-seeking will slip away"

A continuation of the former point. The thesaurus definition of self-seeking is; "self-centered, self-regarding, egocentric, egoistic" Unfortunately, AA members are encouraged to interpret this in the most damaging way. As in religious cults, this "self-seeking" behaviour is seen as detrimental to the group. Sacrifice of self is mandatory if "we" are to transcend ourselves to live a better life. In an altruistic sense, this can be understood as a very humanitarian phrase, but it does not translate as such in AA where hierarchies of "service time" and "sobriety years" act as clear markers of who has the most power. Sponsors with long "clean-time" and who have many sponsees are some of the most controlling and unpleasant people I have ever met.

Being self-regarding and egocentric are essential in some part to maintaining a solid sense of one's own character and personality in a world that does not always respect the individual or our differences. These traits help us to stand up for ourselves and also to reject conformist thinking if we feel it is harmful to our wellbeing.

This simplistic AA slogan marks us out as "selfish" in a pejorative way. You must always put the group first! I have very often had to put my needs in the forefront in order to not only survive but also to progress. And isn't progress to a healthier life what it's all about?

"Our whole attitude and outlook upon life will change"

At the start of my induction into AA (for that is what it was), this phrase really scared me. I liked the way I looked at life, through my own creative lens. I liked my outlook, generally in the political and philosophical senses. This edict tells you that you will be changed by your involvement with this organisation, (and they delivered on that one).

Again, it is "our" not "your". "You" are considered as one of many, of the "tribe" (members often refer to AA as their "tribe") and it reads like a directive more than a suggestion. AA loves saying that these phrases are "suggestions". I disagree with that after years of experience of their brain-washing techniques.

"Fear of people and of economic insecurity will leave us"

My least favourite promise. Monumental hogwash. I BECAME more fearful of people and institutions by being part of AA for many reasons. Primarily, the inappropriate behaviour of many of the men, the "clicky" and malicious gossip of many of the women, the immaturity and unkindness shown toward people in difficult and complex life situations (particularly in the relationship of sponsor/sponsee), and the general shallowness of connections. I never found meetings havens of friendship or safety. To be cautious when meeting new people is a natural response, especially if you have experienced a lot of trauma/abuse.

The part about economic insecurity just floors me. Concern about finances has never left me. I noticed, early on, that the people who most enthusiastically espoused this promise were well-provided for.

I'm a working-class woman and money has always been an issue. I feel relatively ok about it now, but AA did not help that part of my life one iota. Unless of course the promise alludes to the many AA marriages that involve hitch-ups between sugar Daddies and Mummies and Golddiggers (there are many of those). This promise is not worth a pen stroke.

"We will intuitively know how to handle situations which used to baffle us"

Not true. Before AA I had good intuition and could be very confident in some situations; drink didn't always make a difference to that. Life is baffling in a thousand ways for everyone, drunk or not. What I noticed in AA, right from the start, was that any success I had formerly achieved in any area of my life was dismissed as "the overconfidence of the alcoholic", and any success I claimed for myself since joining the fellowship was put down entirely to "the programme" and how it had "worked" on me despite myself! Rubbish.

I agree that I had often made a hash of things when I was drunk, but my sense of fair play and values at work and with friends was not impaired when I was abstinent, in between spells of heavy drinking. I had, and have, a good moral compass. I have many skills and capabilities. "Making amends" is a very human skill that develops with maturity, but does not have to mean abject prostration or crippling guilt-induced apologies, which AA encourages.

AA constantly tells you that you are "baffled" by life in sobriety, but only AA and the fellowship can help you construct and maintain a life of good conduct towards yourself and others. Manipulative and false. With the aid of good counselling and therapy, I have proved to myself that I do not need AA or any other authoritarian group structure to give me "guidelines" for my life.

"We will suddenly realize that God is doing for us what we could not do for ourselves"

There it is. The God bit, the religion, the higher power. Firstly, I don't believe in god. Secondly, I didn't "suddenly realize" anything. Change and self-awareness comes after months and years of self-reflection and seeking, with input and help along the way. There is the "promise" here of an epiphanic religious awakening that we can only experience if we "surrender to a God of our understanding". This is the holy seal of all cult organisations. Once more, the "we" not the "you". I had my own realization and understanding without god or AA, and that continues.

Finally, the summing up paragraph at the end of the "promises" literature.

"Are these extravagant promises? We think not (these three words are echoed by those gathered) They are being fulfilled among us – sometimes quickly, sometimes slowly. They will always materialize if we work for them"

Let's break that down;

"Are these extravagant promises?" – this is the loaded question asked by the confident snake-oil salesman as he concludes his pitch to the gullible. He is assured that he has got you where he wants you; ready to part with your cash and your time for his life-saving formula.

"We think not." – (don't worry! It works!)

"They are being fulfilled among us, sometimes quickly, sometimes slowly" – (this stuff may work for some folks but AA is not taking any responsibility for those who find it completely useless).

"They will always materialize if we work for them"- (if it doesn't work for you, you just haven't worked the programme hard enough and you have failed miserably).

That concluding paragraph is really the pill that the sugar coating of the other promises disguises. Many people relapse on this paragraph alone, unable to accept that their human frailties and vulnerabilities will never be acknowledged in any practical way by AA.

The work ethic and religious stance conveyed here are harsh. The "tough love" of AA and surrender of will to a higher power, or god, presents a hardline, formal religious dogma that leaves you in no doubt as to where you stand (or kneel).

The promises of AA should add "You are either with us, or against us; there is no other way to go forward". It is very black and white.

The promise I now make to myself, and have done for some time, is that I will continue to question the assumed authority, in any organisation, over a person's life. (I got a great deal of practice in this when I was on my cancer treatment programme) Salvation in the form of a rigid, inflexible "programme" is not a promise. It is a loss of personal freedom and agency, costing millions their ability to empower themselves in order to be truly "precious and free" (CODA phrase).

Freedom from alcohol dependency is not the sole domain of AA, and their "promises" are hollow.

Chapter 10

Recovered

In AA, when you introduce yourself as a "recovering alcoholic", you are instantly labelling yourself as someone who can never get well. From the start, I wanted to just be able to say my name and not add the label, it never felt right. However, the consensus of the meeting and of the structure of AA means you are never recovered, always recovering.

During Zoom/Covid, I thought a lot about this. I have many friends and acquaintances from the performing and music worlds, many of whom have struggled at times with drink and drugs; a lot them very high functioning and managing to play or perform with nothing more than muscle memory and a good push onto the stage.

I knew very few who were part of any fellowship programmes which often surprised me. How were they doing it? Not all of them had terrible lives of hell and misery. Many were just occasional boozers or smokers and their lives were very full and mainly happy. Some just went cold turkey and literally never drank or used again, some went to therapy. Few went to AA. (Or maybe they just kept quiet about it, being anonymous...)

I'm intrigued as to why certain people (me included) stick at things when the reality shows that the reward or benefit is simply no longer worth the time and trouble, if it ever was. The short answer for me was that my family background had a lot to do with it. Dysfunction and a lot of hurt paved the stony path to much of my drinking. I had the usual "outsider" character of someone deep into music, theatre, reading and philosophical thought.

The longer answer includes years of therapy and self-help books/workshops, odd career choices/relationships, and the consequential getting to grips with what had turned me toward drink, drugs, sex, food, as ways to fix or control how desperate I felt. In other words, trauma-based drinking/using was my template.

By tackling it and accepting help, I was able to start to move forward. Yet, even with all this awareness and change, I still held on to the AA attachment, many years after I felt it was useful. In fact, I continued going when I knew it was doing me harm. Here, I will point out the good things I initially got from AA. These are things that are common outcomes of joining any new group of people.

1. *Connection to other people who were struggling – I no longer felt alone without the drink.*
2. *Routine; at first, I had no job, no relationship, no real roots in anything permanent other*

than music/performance, and I knew I needed stability.
3. *New friends – I had let go of most of my old drinking mates.*

Yet, I have to say that I did not forge close or lasting friendships with any AA members; I found many damaged people and also a huge number of sanctimonious ones; people I would have avoided like the plague even when I was drinking. I did not belong, but I was willing to see if it would help get my life "back on track".

I can now see that I did not know my "sober self" that well and I had very poor boundaries, being too open with my sharing at times and at others just closing down completely. This is very common on entering the fellowship world. I was encouraged to "share, share, share!", while at the same time being told to "listen and identify with the similarities".

My boundaries improved, but not because of AA; I realised that my sense of self seemed to disappear when I entered "the rooms". After 10 years in the AA/Coda fellowships I no longer needed or wanted to be there and was forging many new connections outside "the rooms". After all, the AA literature does cite AA as a "bridge to normal living". In fact, it is the North Circular on the "road to recovery" map, or maybe Spaghetti Junction….

I did know by this time, that AA was not about "recovery"; it was about conforming to a set of rules ("suggestions") that got regularly bent out of shape by all the sick and manipulative people that came through its doors.

That is when it became difficult for me to identify myself as an "alcoholic". I remember one lunchtime meeting in Bristol; it was busy, about 25 people, all ages, mainly men. A young man came in, he was in his early twenties, and sat next to me. He was bursting to share and when he did, he identified himself as "an alcoholic, addict, overeater, bulimic, gambler, sex addict, borderline personality disordered person in recovery", something along those lines….

At first, I thought he was taking the piss, but no, he was deadly serious and continued to share a long, self-flagellating account of his miserable weekend in a deader than dead-pan monotone. In fact, the chairperson had to cut in and ask him to bring his share to a close as it was a large meeting. He left before the closing prayer and I never saw him again. The swing door kept on swinging. He obviously was in need of help, but not from 12 step programmes.

Labels can be helpful, particularly in the "system" of healthcare that demands specific diagnosis by a qualified health professional in order to access services. Alcoholics are often named as such by treatment centre staff (not always appropriately qualified) who are completely enamoured of the 12-step programme disease model.

It does not work very well in practice; to some extent the harm of labelling is not fully understood until later, when you may want the "labels" removed.

I wanted insurance for musical equipment and travelling; I had admitted I was an "alcoholic" on the form. This led to them requiring an HIV test from me before they would consider my application. Afterwards, my doctor told me that this was now "on the record" and would make it difficult for me to get other types of insurance/loans etc. (the test was negative, but that makes no difference to the insurance companies).

Over my 34 years in AA, I have told dentists, doctors and a legion of health professionals that I am in "recovery" from alcoholism and would always be an "alcoholic". It is in my notes and I have not yet managed to get those labels taken off my case notes. The label given me was by a 12-step religious programme with no scientific evidence to prove that I was, indeed "addicted" to drinking (apart from the "chronic alcoholic curve" diagram that I was shown on my first day in treatment by the resident Doctor).

It is the curse of the "disease" model. Even when you have stopped drinking, the label in your notes will give nurses and doctors pause for thought and many will judge you as weak, unstable and unreliable. I know, because it has happened to me many times. It affects the way you are treated.

In the last few months in AA, attending via Zoom, I began to introduce myself as "I'm Marilyn" and then just plunged into what I wanted to share. No one picked me up on it, but the non-verbal clues of severe disapproval were there, even with the fuzzy screens. When I could no longer bear to hear myself speak the cult-coded language, I left. I was shunned almost immediately – as I expected to be. A few AA members stay in touch; one is a woman I would have called a friend from the word go and she stayed close to me during my cancer.

I met hundreds of women and men in my AA sojourn. I've never felt close to more than a handful – and as I age, I believe if you can count the number of good friends you have on one hand, then you are indeed a very lucky person. Many of those people I met in AA probably left and recovered and went on to live full and productive lives, there are no records. I feel similarly about my cancer recovery.

The haematology consultant I had, said that he hoped he wouldn't be seeing me again, when I left the hospital after my final transplant. We laughed and I realised then that he had probably seen hundreds of people on the cancer ward, many of whom did not make it back out through the hospital doors. A "label" of "cancer survivor" is not something I particularly cherish. I see myself as a person who had cancer, I did not fight a battle with it, nor did I see it as a punishment for being somehow defective. It is part of my history, there is no getting away from that; but the place it takes in my life must be subordinate to the full and loving life I can live now.

Recovered people are not very profitable in the treatment business. I am heartened by the amount of people now leaving 12-step fellowship programmes who are finding other resources to help them give up or moderate their drinking and drug use. I don't drink, that's my choice. I don't judge anyone who chooses to drink, practice harm-reduction or use medications to control cravings. What matters is independent, creative solutions to problems, without the overbearing and dogmatic approaches that programmes/cults like AA are still practicing and presenting as the only solution.

Every organisation has its' success and decline arc. The natural ebb and flow of a group process is one that occurs in every hierarchical structure. People will create different "programmes" or formulas for their problems, and scientific research will continue to come up with new medications and health regimes to complement these.

AA is a clapped-out concept that uses religious principles and literature to perpetuate its own structure and also make a lot of money from its stranglehold on treatment centre recovery culture. It was old-hat even when I joined in the 80's and I felt uncomfortable with the misogyny and the patronizing tone of the Big Book right from the first reading.

I never felt the "gratitude" (though I said I did, because I thought that if I repeated it enough times it would happen) and I never wanted what they had; I wanted help to become well, learn resilience and get started on a new life without drinking. I didn't know I was joining a special club that would make me a member forever and one in which I felt invisible. My individuality in those rooms got eroded and eaten up completely at times and there were points at which I did feel suicidal, something I had never experienced when I was drinking/using drugs.

I dealt with a lot of those issues in therapy and I still have anger towards AA and the "programme"; I have hope that anyone reading this will question and challenge both AA, and their own views on this "anonymous" organisation, which somehow has become acknowledged by media, Hollywood and the court system to be the best way to deal with addiction.

Wrong. However, they get great coverage everywhere from celebrities in all areas of life, eager to tell everyone about their anonymous recovery to anyone who will listen.

Here are the Oxford dictionary definitions of "recover";

> *"Find, get back, recapture, restore, retrieve, salvage, trace, track down, win back, rally, recuperate, regain one's strength, pull through, revive, survive, take a turn for the better"*

All these terms mean more to me now that I have left AA. The coded, short-cut language that AA uses dismisses the in-depth meaning and vitality of someone's lived experience and I am weeding this jargon out of my vocabulary. Like most people leaving a cult-like structure, I do sometimes find myself thinking "in slogans". I take a deep breath and blow it away and realise it will take time before I am completely free of the "marketing hooks" and acronyms.

Daily repetitions and meetings ensured that I constantly monitored myself for faults and failings. I rarely do that now, unless something specific "triggers" me when I am in a new situation or facing a difficult challenge, maybe a confrontation with authorities of some kind or a face-to-face meeting with someone that doesn't go to plan and becomes uncomfortable (this happens much less since I left AA, because I don't "second-guess" the other person and wonder how I am going to square it all with my 10th step...)

I am recovered from the need/desire/compulsion to be in a group of people who;

> 1. *Show no authentic desire to get to know who I am, other than the fact that I used to drink and use drugs to cope with life and want to stay sober "just for today".*
> 2. *Who only see me, ultimately, as a resource to recruit new membership to a self-perpetuating structure that is, at its' roots, conservative, religious, outdated and failing its objective (though if, as I believe, its objective is to turn out conformist, unquestioning people who have lost the ability to think critically and are unable to cope with change or challenge, and must always look fearfully toward a "higher*

power" in order to live, then I have to say that AA has been an unqualified success). In whose interests does AA want me as a "grateful recovering alcoholic"? You may well ask.

Goodbye to all that.

Chapter 11
Unlearning

My first 2 years in AA recovery was my "honeymoon period. The time of open disclosure (too much invariably), group coffee get-togethers, instant attachments that I thought might be long-lasting (they weren't) and an overload of meetings. I believe there is a parallel here with what we learn in our first two years of life. The attachments we make in our families map out how we are able to cope (or not) in the world once we have left home or begin to make our way in the world.

Depending on your own experience, AA can feel like a familiar place, maybe a hostile one, but the important thing is the familiarity. AA breaks you open with "love" or "love bombing" as it is known. Instant availability, open communication (seemingly); you feel understood and accepted for the first time in years. You have a support network that you can go to or call on at any time, and it's free! If you are working class and have little "cash" behind you from your family, then this package comes over as very appealing.

It works for a while, particularly at the very beginning when you are needy, suggestible and have nowhere else to turn. That 2-year "cloud 9" period ended for me when I was repeatedly let down, then dumped by my 13th stepping AA boyfriend, as well as being on the receiving end of a lot of bullying and toxic behaviour from group members, particularly women.

A huge wave of grief engulfed me for many months after the unhealthy relationship with Derek ended. Wellsprings of emotion about my childhood, my relationships and my miscarriage just kept on flooding through me. I was at a point of raw vulnerability.

However, AA did me a great deal of harm at this point as I got little support from the groups I attended, and the women were the worst "comforters", reminding me very much of my Mother and my sister. I was just "too much", and was constantly encouraged to "let go and move on". I was not capable of doing this without help. That was when I accessed intensive therapy from my local mental health team to deal with these core trauma issues.

Qualified health professionals helped me pick up the fragments and I did not drink or take drugs. I still felt all the pain, particularly at AA meetings where I felt I had to put on a shiny face and spew out the programme mantras. Many people aren't as lucky as I was; access to mental health services was a good deal easier in 1980's UK.

I was caught up in using the AA jargon throughout my time in the fellowships. Naturally, it is easier to communicate when you know the coded language in any culture. Yet the way AA members talk and reject "outsiders" or "normals" is very excluding and makes it very cult-like. Many of my old friends were very concerned when I got deeply involved in AA at the start; some even suggested that I had no drinking problem and certainly could not be called an alcoholic.

I vehemently disagreed; I wanted the label, I wanted to have a proper explanation for my confused state of mind that had pushed me to drink so heavily for so long. I am very self-willed, something that AA spends a great deal of time shaming you about until you are broken down and accept your "powerlessness".

I think this is dangerous. I had to unlearn "I am powerless" thoroughly, once I realised that it was keeping me inhibited and fearful on a daily basis. But initially I ignored my friends concerns and ploughed on ahead with this "new way of living". I drifted away from everyone I had hung out with (some were very old friends). I regret that now.

They were trying to get me to take time to consider what I was enmeshed in. I didn't listen. I did have a heavy drinking problem; I had no argument with that. But AA was not the best place for me to deal with that. I didn't know any better and was too trusting of those AA members I got involved with and the authority figures who pushed me toward the decision to go into treatment. I was 30, but more like a 16-year-old in many ways.

I believed that the AA network was holding me up and keeping me sober. The clever lie of AA is that after 2 years, you need never "think" about your drinking issues again in a conscious way. The programming does it for you. My very first meeting in London, left me with the deep impression that AA was a "crutch" and I did not want to rely on it forever – my intuition was correct, but I pushed it down.

For example, when I was at college in Bath, a group of fellow performing arts students invited me out for a drink and then a party – pretty tame stuff compared with what I had been used to in my former "drinking life" (AA encourages you to think you have had "two lives"; one drunk and one sober). I refused the invitation, thereby cutting myself out of what turned out to be a fun evening from all accounts. I had instead, left college at 4pm, gone to Waitrose to buy a microwaveable meal and caught the bus home to the cottage I was renting a room in outside of town. I spent the evening working and felt thoroughly miserable. But I was sober!

What had happened in my brain when I was asked to go out with my friends and have a good time? My mind had instantly clicked into AA 12 step mode. Something like this; "this is risky, one drink is too many and a thousand is never enough; you won't be able to control yourself; follow the thought of the drink through to the gutter where you will surely end up; a moments' pleasure, a lifetime of pain that will inevitably lead to jails, institutions and death; get to a meeting, call your sponsor, you are powerless…." All this in seconds. PROGRAMMED!

I have had many similar examples where I excused or absented myself from enjoyable outings and situations. I slowly reversed this process over the years, because, by nature I have a lot of courage, resilience and a huge lust for life (again, AA discourages this, calling it "ego run rampant") Even AA cannot suppress this forever. Not in me anyway!

Yet it can do lasting damage when a vulnerable person needs support, care and guidance in getting control and power back into their lives, or they want to continue drinking or using drugs in moderation. AA's counter argument would go something like this; "But Marilyn, the programme worked for you! It saved you from yourself, you have the steps to thank for that, and ultimately God". As for drinking in moderation; they would say that, in that case, you were never a "real alcoholic" to begin with.

I was inside that structure for many years, looking out – and "out" became much more attractive as time went on. I was still going to meetings, chanting the slogans, counting the birthdays and proclaiming AA to be the saviour of many a drunk, including me (I never gave that accolade to god as I didn't believe in one, or rather I didn't believe in any deity that AA would promote)

Back in my rented room, alone I was faced with deep-seated emotional pain, abandonment issues and losses of connection to family and friends. My music and my writing got me through the worst of it. I became more skilled in the subjects I had chosen; I worked hard at my "craft" and took on some small roles in avant-garde music/theatrical events, I did poetry readings with a women's' group which was great fun and liberating.

 I grew and I changed. I did not share much of this artistic life at AA or Coda meetings. The cult of the individual was frowned upon. I lived a double life as I unlearned the messages from treatment and old-time AA "gurus".

I explored mysticism, spiritualism, macrobiotics, yoga, tai chi, massage, Alexander technique, 5 rhythms dancing, reiki, colour therapy, sound baths, Buddhism, Osho, Gurdjieff and Ouspensky, Jung, Perls; you name it, I had a good look at it! AA could not and never would be a place where I would be able to grow, change and challenge their ideas and concepts. It is a closed shop.

In some ways, I used it as a dysfunctional family; somewhere I could always return to for a dollop of critical, shame inducing "advice". For trauma-bonded people (of which I am one), the familiarity of abuse plays a large part in this unhealthy connection. I was attracted equally to what hurt and what healed me.

The trick I had to learn, was to sort out the conflicting messages, say yes to the good ones and a big, fat NO to the destructive ones. That took me years. When anyone asks me why I stayed in AA for so long, I have to reply; "how long is a piece of string?". The question is futile in the context of a situation where someone's mental state has been manipulated over time and with deliberation, to such a degree that white is black and vice versa (though the subtleties are infinitely greater than that).

This then begs the question; why do so many people outside of AA (i.e., those who have never attended meetings) believe it to be the best method for helping people with alcohol/drug misuse issues? If it works for some people (millions, it is claimed by AA) then that is good, isn't it? Maybe, but there is evidence that only 5-8% of people using AA as a recovery programme benefit in the long-term. Most people coming through the doors of AA leave after a year. Surely that suggests a deeper study of what is going on is needed? Or is it just much easier for society to toss the "drunks and the junkies" into profitable treatment centres, (usually 12-step fellowship based) and AA meetings and forget about them? (AA is free at point of use, but don't forget that your dollar or pound goes into the pot and ultimately to AA World Service Inc.; that is a whole lot of "pots" by the way, for those people who think that AA is a non-profit organisation).

This approach is much easier than addressing the underlying issues of poverty, trauma, abuse, homelessness, lack of education or opportunities, mental illness and many other issues; the list is long and not many people in governments seem interested. The only thing governments seem keen on is "the war on drugs" which as history has shown us, is a continuous, ridiculous money-hole maintained by the wrong set of people, and it doesn't work.

Following treatment, the 12-step fellowship carousel of endless meetings awaits……. the money mounts up and is dutifully sent to "intergroup" and thence to the regional office…. ultimately AA World service office employs highly paid executives and other staff, plus "Grapevine inc", the publishing arm of AA produces a forests worth of AA literature – which you can buy….

Not many people connect the dots on this. I didn't for many years. I didn't even know that AA was a registered charity for many years. It is now easy to donate to AA at the click of a button online. Cash donations are kept to a limit; but who is monitoring how many times someone clicks the button under different names or accounts? Where is the regulatory body that looks into AA's amassed wealth as a charity that should be publicly scrutinized?

AA treatment centres have a near-monopoly when it comes to addiction services. Society needs to unlearn the sacred dogma that pushes AA as the main pathway to life as a recovered alcoholic/addict (if you so choose to call yourself).

My "unlearning" is ongoing. I no longer feel empty when I think about AA – I used to feel bad when I had missed a meeting….and then I went 13 years without any and I was fine! (Again, AA would dispute that and tell me that either I wasn't a "real" alcoholic or I wasn't actually fine at all; "fucked-up, insecure, neurotic and egotistical" was one acronym thrown at me in some smoke-filled church room many years ago….)

Certain situations and "triggers" can sometimes still lead me into a mindset where I start to remember AA and I begin to embellish the memory through rose-coloured glasses. I follow that thought through; a zoom meeting of mainly strangers (I am still shielding), no authentic discussion or interaction, disconnection between shares (i.e., no reflective thinking/feedback; yet you'll get plenty of "advice" after the meeting), coded language that reduces and denigrates real, lived experiences and emotional responses; an empty feeling once the meeting is over (despite most people saying what a wonderful meeting it was), no sense of a holding, safe environment.

Even in physical meetings (face to face) before Covid/cancer, I never felt safe. Anyone can walk into an AA meeting; all you have to do is admit you have a drinking problem; therefore, vulnerable people need to have boundaries in place (and many don't). Predatory people are legion in fellowship meetings. I've gone backwards in some ways; I have less trust of new people and groups and I'm realising how healthy that now feels to me. I've learned that "drama" and the toxic atmosphere of gossip and criticism no longer appeals to me.

All this is prevalent in AA meetings and is never addressed at the "group conscience" meeting. If someone does challenge the "group think", they are quickly dismissed or voted down by the toxic minority who have taken over the group by stealth. The only "protection" for members anonymous status is the famed "yellow card"! "Who you see hear, what you hear here, when you leave here, let it stay here" It is rarely, if ever, honoured, and now in the 21st century and internet overload, nothing remains unknown for long.

Watching YouTube clips of people who have left cults such as scientology and countless others, I was struck by the resonance I felt with them. Some had been born into a cult or been there most of their lives. Having left, not only are they "shunned" by the organisations, they are also left in an extremely vulnerable position, having to navigate a world that they do not understand or feel "normal" in. It can take years of focused therapy with experts in the field of "cult exiting" for the person to begin a new life, free from the brainwashing of the cult (though in many cases, it never completely disappears).

I'm very "grateful" (hard for me to use that word due to it being weaponized by the fellowship) that I didn't find AA until I was 30. Increasingly, younger people are going to AA (there is also Al-a-teen for even younger members); young people of 18 and 19 years old are still, obviously, experimenting with life in many ways – alcohol and drugs are usually "rites of passage" for the majority of young adults. They are also very malleable and a label of "addict" at 18 is a very powerful message to the self.

My own family used my "alcoholic" label when it suited them to saddle me with all manner of unearned guilt and shame, my sister in particular, from whom I remain estranged. I was the "scapegoat" in my family in childhood and into later years. The AA tag compounded the guilt – "hey, you are an alcoholic! Of course, we can't trust you/help you/believe you – oh and it's all your fault! (Whatever the situation was). This continued throughout my 30's and 40's. The trap within the trap as it were.

By making a geographical move when my husband suffered a major heart attack at a relatively young age, I was able to reset my life and pull back my own power by putting distance between myself and my family of origin. This made a huge difference to our lives and was not the negative event that AA members continually bang on about i.e., "doing a geographical". In AA parlance this means moving around to avoid being "responsible". I was considered foolish for making the move and received little or no support; luckily by then I had very little contact with AA and was able to plan and execute the move with no feelings of guilt or shame for doing the "wrong thing". This move marked my 13-year disconnection from AA and CODA.

On the subject of "wrong things" I want to mention inappropriate disclosure and how big a part it has in the daily damage being done by 12 step fellowship groups. I cringe when I recall some of the personal, intimate information that I have shared in open, mixed meetings. There are no boundaries, no safeguards; because no one is in charge! I also heard horrific tales of sustained incest, murder and rape – all within the "safe confines of the rooms". It is appalling.

Treatment cedntre group therapy was similarly open and unregulated. Very damaged people sharing for the first time in their lives about abusive situations to a peer group of individuals they barely knew, managed by another "alcoholic/addict" in recovery who had little or no professionally recognised qualifications (my experience is from the late 80's).

Imagine my cancer consultant coming into my hospital room with a friend who has had a life-long interest in cancer care; they may even have experienced cancer themselves. Then, my consultant leaves me with his friend who is charged with overseeing my treatment in the future……..aghhhhh!

Alcoholism is not an illness. For years I was in two minds about this. The disease model did not make sense when I followed the logic. However, sometimes, when I was at a very low ebb in AA rooms, it felt more comforting to hang onto that disease label; it gave me a certain security, maybe even an excuse, because I had no idea what else I could rely on to help me.

Slowly, that reliance dissipated and I refuted the illness model openly at every opportunity. It didn't make me any friends with the old brigade, but many newcomers came and talked to me after meetings. This awareness contributed increasingly to the feeling I had; "I don't belong here – in fact I don't think I ever did"

After my cancer diagnosis, subsequent treatment/transplant and extreme vulnerability, I found AA zoom meetings to be paper tigers of solace. There was, literally, nothing there that was doing me any good. Each time I attended, I felt like a little part of me had been wounded again. My body was so fragile that I felt this viscerally – a bad headache, nausea, constipation or anxiety would occur directly as a result of attending the meeting. AA was making me sick and I had just got over the most major illness of my life. To hear people talk of the "disease of alcoholism" was enough to make me want to puke after what I had been through.

Unlearning can take a very long time; yet there are also many short, sharp shock moments that elevate understanding and awareness mighty fast. Cancer did that for me. And I listened; carefully.

Chapter 12

Trauma

The Oxford dictionary definition of trauma is; *emotional shock, physical injury; resulting shock*

Being born is our first major trauma. We are shaped continuously by events and our reactions and responses to them. Childhood is traumatic for everyone to a certain degree, but some experience more trauma than others. We carry and deal with our "wounds" in a variety of ways. Thinking you can escape trauma is a kind of "magical thinking" that does not make for resilience in times of growth and change.

In some ways I was over-protected as a child, in other ways I was neglected, particularly in relation to encouragement to be authentic and pursue the activities and interests I was drawn to. I was criticized a great deal; I lacked a healthy connection to my mother, and my sister literally hated me.

 My Dad was always the one I felt I could trust the most, yet even he was very often unavailable due to constant shift work and his own lifelong struggles with depression. This background is neither unusual or highly abusive. But it was hard to be me in my family, and I turned to drink and rash behaviour to compensate for what was missing.

Joining AA at 30, I was told by old-timers that I had done the right thing, that I had reached a "rock bottom" and was in the right place. They seemed so very certain that I felt compelled to believe them. There were many people much younger than me, but we all felt that we were in the same boat, looking up to the elders who had 15,20- and 30-years sober time.

Thirty years seemed unimaginable to me at that time; a position of such sacred status that I wouldn't have dared to speak to a man or woman who had attained such an honourable position in AA. One of the constant mixed-messages of AA is that you are nothing special and different, yet the hierarchy plays out differently.

I was told to "shut your mouth and open your ears" so many times in the first few meetings that it made me extremely shy of saying anything. "Look for the similarities, not the differences" is the other phrase often repeated to newcomers; I've said it myself a thousand times. Nowadays I do the exact opposite, I find it much more reliable for my well-being. A warning bell did go off when I heard it the first time though.

I've always had a strong belief that difference is what makes us interesting. As a performer, I have met an amazing array of disparate people; actors, dancers, musicians, poets, painters of all ages, races, genders and class. I have been lucky to have been involved in creating many theatrical productions and being part of the magic of "making things happen" on the stage. It has been a joyful part of my life. These productions brought with them rehearsals, disagreements, sweat and tears, drawn out discussions, workshops and a hell of a lot of laughs, all essential ingredients of a group working together on a single purpose, but which recognises each persons' individuality.

What I couldn't get used to in AA was the intolerance of difference – in the sense that the 12 steps are akin to the 10 commandments; you dare not question them or challenge them or bring any new ideas to the table. I tried; as thousands of others have done before me and thousands will do in the future.

The consensus rules, but the toxic minority control the structure. The individual must give in, fearful of being ostracized for disagreeing, and the rules stay the same, unchallenged by time, new scientific ideas, or common sense. The difference in a theatrical show is that it is just a show and never promises to be anything else.

  AA has its own roster of promises, and members insist that if you "come round to our way of thinking" you will have all your problems solved. Or, as they like to proclaim; "if you want what we have, you will go to any lengths to get it"

A quick point here; many people will tell you how AA has changed their lives for the better; this includes politicians who make decisions that harm vulnerable sectors of society, deceitful hedge fund managers, domestic abusers, spiteful teachers, the list is endless, these are just examples. But if, at the end of a fraught day, they go to AA, stand up and say "I'm an alcoholic and I didn't drink today" they are clapped and rewarded with a warm glow of acceptance.

Double-standards are at the foundation of the 12-step programmes and always have been. Being a "work in progress" is no excuse for predatory or bullying behaviour. There seems to be an assumption in the media that when someone attends AA, they become an enlightened being.

This is when re-traumatization and CPTSD (complex post traumatic stress disorder) are re-activated. Example; a vulnerable woman with PTSD from abusive relationships/family system and who has used drink and drugs to cope with the physical and emotional pain, comes into the rooms and is told by virtually everyone that it is safe there and that in order to get well, she must "trust and have faith in the programme" and the people in the rooms. She is at a very low ebb, but feels she has few options; she is desperate.

However, she is also very intelligent and asks many questions in those first 6 meetings (AA suggests you attend 6 meetings, sit and listen and then make up your mind about staying) You will be given phone numbers and those people will very likely contact you between meetings and encourage you to work the programme and to keep returning to the rooms.

Continuing with the scenario; an older female AA member takes the woman aside after the meeting and tells her she is really angry and should be dealing with that and offers to sponsor her; at another meeting, an older man confides inappropriate incest survivor information over coffee in a secluded corner of the church hall; another young woman offers to give her a massage (the woman can barely stand to be touched); a young man, a "newcomer", follows her home, talking incessantly and wanting to go into her flat for coffee, she finds it too hard to say no and he eventually forces himself upon her and she is too ashamed to tell anyone in her family.

However, she does tell her AA sponsor, who advises her to look at "her part" in the encounter and then to make amends with the young man. The sponsor advises her to keep it within AA and not to take it to the police as they would not understand how AA operates and it would compromise anonymity.

This flood of confusing experiences (and many more) continues throughout the 6 meetings. At the end of them, the woman is bewildered and experiences powerful "flashbacks", reliving her painful experiences. She feels ashamed and deeply troubled. At no point does anyone suggest she seek help other than an AA meeting.

But she has managed to stay sober, for which she is congratulated. In AA, this is a success story. Her damage has been relived and intensified and no real practical help offered, and the woman is very likely to relapse at this point.

All these incidents have happened, I have been made aware of them or have witnessed them. That makes me part of it too, I understand that. It is the main reason I am writing this book. What would help? AA would argue that the situation I have described is unfairly portrayed; it could happen in any group situation, e.g., a walking club, a cookery class, an online chat group etc. Yes, it could, and having poor boundaries in any group can lead to trouble very quickly, particularly for women.

There's the rub; AA professes to be a self-help fellowship; however, it is also a registered charity with a duty of care to safeguarding those who come through its many doors. It is accountable to the taxman and should also be publicly transparent as to its success rates and details of criminal incidents reported by members. But it isn't. Let's look at Tradition 4 of AA;

Each group should be autonomous except in matters affecting other groups or AA as a whole.

If I interpret this correctly, this means AA is responsible for the activities of group members within its structure and if criminal acts are committed, they need to investigate them and call in police help when appropriate.

Treatment centres founded on 12-step fellowship programmes make thousands in profits, yet sustained recovery figures are poor and many people go "through" treatment multiple times, using up life-savings, hard-earned salaries and loans from distraught family members. Treatment centres have become the "honey pots" of alcohol/drug "care". Also, when they leave treatment, people suddenly realise that they can get everything they got at the centres for free – at 12 step fellowship meetings in the community!

My own trauma became apparent very quickly in AA and I was fortunate to go to a qualified professional outside of its claustrophobic rooms. The "magical thinking" I refer to is a by-product of fear; a coping mechanism and an avoidance of reflective thought.

It is easier to "hand over" your will and your life (as AA "suggests") and then go for a coffee or a walk and believe you have "done the work" than it is to dig deep and rely on your own resources. Your own inner power does all the work that AA claims for itself.

How often have I heard the following? "I was completely baffled, so I got down on my knees and prayed and handed it over. When I woke the next day, it was as if a lightbulb had turned on; I had a spiritual awakening! God had done for me what I couldn't do for myself" *I've heard it thousands of times.*

Picture the woman I describe walking into an AA meeting and hearing this for the first time. She may think she has walked into a religious revivalist meeting. She may feel hope, relief, fear, mistrust; at that moment she is experiencing a critical turning point that could bring her to a place of reaching out for much needed help. She will get telephone numbers and slogans aplenty; "don't pick up that first drink, pick up the phone", "keep it simple", "one day at a time".

During Covid/zoom meetings, when any young woman came onto a meeting sounding traumatized and fearful, I would privately message them and encourage them to seek professional help and also mention other harm-reduction models of treatment and books about alcohol misuse that I had read, not based on fellowship programmes.

What I was doing was in contradiction of AA principles, but they were my principles which had long been sublimated to the AA dogmatic programme. I feel that similar re-direction would have been so very helpful to me when I first joined AA, not the Big Book of nonsense.

Let there be no confusion about this; AA specifically and categorically instructs its members (or "suggests" as they would have it) to "put principles before personalities". The sub-text of this coded language is "AA principles matter more than your intuitive responses". I will end this chapter with some points that outline practices which I believe intensify trauma responses in members. (In no particular order of relevance).

1. *No public accountability; (it is difficult to obtain statistics from AA treatment centres about success rates, relapses, suicides or re-admissions*
2. *No formalized qualification is required to work with alcoholic/drug misuse patients.*
3. *"One size fits all"; fellowship approaches to treatment of alcohol/drug misuse do not inspire confidence in the users, who have individual histories of trauma requiring differing solutions.*

4. *Safeguarding; unregulated, open disclosure is commonplace in meetings and treatment centres. Predatory behaviour is rife.*
5. *Unequal balance of power; "sponsors" and "old-timers" can wield tremendous power over vulnerable newcomers and also keep meetings and members "in-line" when there is controversy or challenge to the group. Bullying, coercive behaviours abound.*
6. *Religious dogma; AA is a religious organisation (despite its protests to the contrary) Many people coming to AA have been abused in religious orders/denominations/cults. AAs second step says "Came to believe that a power greater than ourselves could restore us to sanity"; my translation of that step would be "Became indoctrinated to believe that only god can help us, as we are insane"*
7. *AA does not welcome discussion on other forms of treatment/harm reduction at its meetings. Members on prescription drugs and medication essential to their wellbeing are routinely told by sponsors to stop taking their meds, often leading to dangerous, and sometimes fatal consequences. "Throw the pills away and pray" – I heard this said to a young man taking medication for paranoid schizophrenia.*

8. *Court mandated attendance to AA/NA meetings is an abuse of human rights. Also, it is potentially dangerous if sexual offenders are attending open meetings and their identity is protected from the other members in the group. (Another safeguarding issue).*
9. *Lifetime commitment to AA; You are never cured (how depressing is that assumption!). If you leave, then you are doomed to "jails, institutions and death" as the inevitable outcomes. No hope of long-term success or recovery on your own terms; endless meetings and recruitment of new members, service and confession and amends…. the cycle goes on forever. You are in for the long-haul.*

In my own experience, trauma and heavy drinking went together. My trauma or "attachment disorder" made me vulnerable to drinking as a cure for emotional issues, PTSD and a "frozen" self. I was unable to cultivate healthy patterns of living. AA intensified my low-self-esteem, guilt, shame and need for approval.

When I finally left AA, I began to grieve and find within myself an unshakeable allegiance to my inner self; the loveable child I had always been, and to make a safe space to cry, laugh, rage and progress at my own pace. Without a toxic, judgmental audience. It had been a long time coming, and at last, it felt like I was coming home – to myself.

Chapter 13

Awareness

Oxford dictionary definition; informed, knowledgeable, observant, responsive, sensitive, acquainted with, alive to, appreciative of, awake to, conscious of, conversant with, familiar with, heedful of, mindful of, sensible of, versed in.

Dropping out of the "game" of AA meant walking away from narcissists, bullies and fakers. It meant spending time on myself, with myself, for myself; it felt authentic and positive, a real response to life, rather than a reaction.

"Stockholm Syndrome" is when a hostage or victim identifies positively with their aggressor. When the hostage/victim is released, they often experience PTSD (post traumatic stress syndrome) which can include insomnia, nightmares, flashbacks and lack of trust (even with close family members and friends). I believe my association with AA bears resemblance to this syndrome.

To become a willing participant in your own servitude, with a continuing desire to appease the aggressor, is actually a coping mechanism, usually displayed by someone who is already fragile or vulnerable. You don't have to be "stupid". You have to be unaware.

The close emotional connection to a person or, as in my case with AA, brought a measure of sanity to an unbearable situation. To "learn to live with" a predicament rather than "rebel" in favour of your own good, seems reasonable. Especially if you came from a dysfunctional/abusive background.

Manipulators recognise people with a strongly compassionate nature, which they then use to their benefit in order to make themselves feel "better than". They feel "normal" when others around them are subdued or repressed. It is the secret, silent language of the oppressor (be it a person or a group).

It is the spoiled, narcissistic child trying to control all conditions for its own advantage or convenience. To take the ice shard out of one's heart and escape from the grip of the Snow Queen is not easy; the relative conditions of "safety" and "security" offered by the Queen may seem to outweigh the uncertainty and loneliness of freedom.

Awareness increases intelligence, not knowledge. It fosters maturity and will keep on growing if it is nurtured – only then can the separation be achieved and the self-love can re-enter the heart.

Being "good enough" for myself was a big step in staying away from AA once the big penny had dropped. It isn't up to me to save anyone or "carry the message". If my life gives anyone else hope, then that is a bonus – but I cannot supply meaning for anyone else's life. That is an individual search and it never comes from outside; no group, no person, no higher power, no fantastic material experience can give it to me. Repetition of slogans or mantras will not "enlighten" me.

I choose to look or not to look at what arises in me and make choices accordingly – I don't need a "sponsor" to show me or advise me. Before we know it, we will be on the way out of this life, through that last door which doesn't revolve.

My Dad, on his deathbed, suddenly looked up at me, eyes still bright, despite his wasted body, and said "I can't believe it's gone so quickly!" (He was 85) He sounded like a small boy coming out from the Cinema after watching his favourite double-bill (he was a film fanatic; something I share with him).

It felt like an acknowledgement to the Universe that life, like Spring snow, arrives in a whirlwind and then melts silently in the sun. He died 12 hours later, and I feel he had an "aware" death, even though his illness had been hard and painful (though mercifully short).

Hours wasted on meaningless pastimes, jobs and relationships will come back to haunt us as we age and head back to the stars as dust. I made a decision during my cancer treatment to let go of all that no longer served me. The books I didn't want to read; the people I no longer felt connected with, the groups I no longer wanted to attend. Why waste the precious time?

AA was at the top of that list. The 5-8% success rate of AA continues steadily on. The AA apologists welcome a constant stream of biddable "newcomers", standing up proudly to declare their loyalty to a "programme" that "saved their lives". The 12-step treatment disease model thunders on, churning out robotic "recovery" droids ready to subjugate themselves in "fellowship" life once they leave the centre; "one day at a time". Before they know it, 30 years has swept by. A dictators dream!

The abstinence fixation of the disease model denies thousands of people a decent, recovered life in which they can move away from "programmes" and decide for themselves if they need to abstain from alcohol and drugs or if they can moderate their usage. They can even decide that they are cured. How dangerous that concept is to the business interests of "recovery" clinics!

AA is an extremely well-known organisation that can hardly claim anonymous status in the 21st century. It has become synonymous with an enhanced spirituality, or "awakening" in people who join its ranks. It is embedded, like all institutions, so deeply in our cultural framework that it feels like it has always been there and therefore has a legitimacy that need not be questioned.

Those of us who have left the fellowship programmes challenge this legitimacy and will continue to do so; there are far too many things wrong in AA for it to escape independent public scrutiny indefinitely. The oft-quoted slogan; "It's an honest programme! Get real!" needs to be bounced back to AA. Perhaps a massive overhaul is coming; a re-branding for the internet age, an acknowledgement of failures and unsafe practices...... Or maybe it will just continue to roll on; the wagon of alcoholism speeding along until the last wonky wheel falls off.

There will always be alcohol and drug use and misuse. My hope is that there will be an ever-growing movement to de-stigmatize people who seek help if they need to and that the services available to them will be tailored to their individual requirements.

 I visualize that the power and prestige of AA's "wagon" will come to a large roundabout with many exits and it will be forced down the "rue sans issue". AA became a one-way street for me, it didn't hear me, it didn't see me, it didn't heal me. It certainly didn't cure me or save my life. I no longer feel the pull of its ancient engine. I wish you all a safe journey.

The End

Printed in Great Britain
by Amazon